# Far from Home

# Far from Home

## Memories of World War II and Afterward

## Mary Herring Wright

Gallaudet University Press
*Washington, D.C.*

Gallaudet University Press
Washington, D.C. 20002
http://gupress.gallaudet.edu

Front cover photograph of Mary Herring Wright, courtesy of the author.
Front cover photograph of view down Pennsylvania Avenue, Washington, D.C.,
courtesy of the Library of Congress, Prints and Photographs Division,
Theodor Horydczak Collection [LC-H8-CT-A02 DLC (color corrected film copy slide)].

Library of Congress Cataloging-in-Publication Data

Wright, Mary Herring, 1924–
    Far from home : memories of World War II and afterward / Mary Herring Wright.
    p. cm.
    ISBN 1-56368-319-9 (alk. paper)
    1. Wright, Mary Herring, 1924–   2. Deaf women—Washington (D.C.)—Biography.
3. African American women—Washington (D.C.)—Biography.   I. Title.
HV2534.W75W75 2005
362.4′2′092—dc22                                                          2005040031

# Contents

# Far from Home

# 1

# A Trip North

A *slumber did my spirit seal;*
*I had no human fears:*
*She seemed a thing that could not feel*
*The touch of earthly years.*

William Wordsworth,
"A Slumber Did My Spirit Seal"

THE BUS droned along the highway on its way to Washington, D.C. I watched the peaceful countryside roll by, with banks on each side covered with shortleaf pine and cedar trees and patches of snow here and there. Could this really be me, Mary Herring, not even a year out of school, who had never traveled this far alone before? I had never planned this.

The summer of 1942 had been spent about like the rest of my summers in Iron Mine, North Carolina, working on the farm, following my sister Eunice when and wherever I could and enjoying having two little nieces to play with, Della and Maxine. Then Papa's cousin Mary Fennell, from Washington, D.C., came for a visit. I'd never met her. We took to each other right away. She was large and comfortable and very nice-looking. My deafness didn't faze her at all. She told Mama and Papa about the special hospital up there just for ear, eye, nose, and throat ailments and

1

that they should send me up there the first chance they got, and she'd get me tested and see if anything could be done about my hearing. Neither Papa nor I paid that much mind, but I could see that Mama had found hope. She did so much want me to hear, but I had decided long ago to make the best of my life, one way or the other. My hearing went very gradually when I was in the fourth grade. At first it was hard to communicate with hearing people but I kept talking and learned to read lips. Some people would write me notes. If pen and paper were not available, some people would take my hand and trace the words on to it.

Although Eunice was married and supposedly living in Richmond, Virginia, she was home as much as she was up there. I'd been visiting her when Cousin Mary said for me to come to Washington. So, here I was, on my way to the city. The construction jobs that Eunice's husband went on often took him to out-of-the-way places, and she would spend those times at home.

My thoughts turned to the past summer and home. I had missed Queen, my pet dog, terribly at first, but I gradually got used to being without her. Only when I'd wander about the fields and go out to the pond did it seem that she was still trotting along with me. The bus stopped to pick someone up, and I looked out the window. I was always interested in new places when I would see them. After the newest passenger was settled, the bus started up again, and so did my thoughts of home and the past few months. In spite of the war, it had been a happy summer and fall of 1942. When it was time to return to Raleigh and the North Carolina School for the Blind and Deaf, I felt funny, sort of misplaced or something, and I missed the kids and Miss Watford, in fact, the whole campus. I think what I missed most was the ease with which I could join in a conversation, know what was being said, and put in my two cents' worth. Now I was back to looking in on conversations and guessing, unless Mama or Sam spelled

Me and Jessie Cooley in 1941.

it out for me. Some of the girls in the crowd, mainly Gladys, Doris, Edna, and Otelia Hayes, would keep me informed. I'd had two other friends who'd do that, but they had moved away. Berthena had moved to Philadelphia, where she'd had a nice wedding and married her longtime sweetheart, Johnny Rea. The other girl was Lena Mae, who I believe went to New York. But mostly, I kept a paperback suspense story handy to read while others talked. I would even take it to the table at mealtime. I knew that was ill-mannered, but I wanted something to keep my mind busy.

I'd had several letters from my friends Hill and Flossie. New leaders had since taken the place of our old gang. Flossie led the girls in signing songs. Maybur was a big wheel also. Madga had married Don, and they lived in Brooklyn. My last steady, Sonny, had also moved there. I still got letters from him. Jessie lived in Springfield, Massachusetts. Margie lived in Philadelphia, Pennsylvania. Ethel was still in Goldsboro, North Carolina. I didn't know if any of the others had married or not. The changes made me feel a little sad for bygone school days, but I was glad. They all seemed happy with their new lives. My mind touched on marriage and quickly jumped off again. That was something I couldn't even imagine for myself, and frankly, I wanted no part of it.

Again, I looked out the window at the Virginia countryside. It was different from North Carolina, with lots of fir and cedar trees, shortleaf pines, and less underbrush. I noticed, too, that my fellow passengers were beginning to stir around, getting things together and putting on their coats. Looking at my watch I saw it was near the time I'd been told we would reach Washington. I hastily gathered up my few belongings, some magazines and snacks, and put on my coat and a beanie hat that was a leftover from school. I then kept my face to the window, waiting to catch my first glimpse of Washington. It wasn't too long in coming. First, I saw scattered buildings and streetlights, then we were on a bridge crossing a wide river, and from there I could see the tall tip of the Washington Monument on one side and I recognized the Jefferson Monument on the other side along with the cherry trees. My brother Willie had taken pictures of them during the summer he'd spent with Cousin Mary. I'd never thought of going to Washington. I'd imagined what it would be like to live in New York City, and even London or Paris, far-off places, but never D.C. Now here I was, riding into it, and all alone at that.

The bus was going through streets now and I was tied up in knots. Suppose I couldn't find Cousin Mary in the waiting room. What would I do? I'd never been in a place like Washington before. Outside the window I saw a street sign saying New York Avenue, N.W., then a large building. The bus was coming to a stop. The people up front were already standing, waiting for the door to open. Pretty soon I was off the bus and following my fellow passengers into the waiting room, and there right near the door sat Cousin Mary. She'd already seen me and was smiling a welcome. After hugging me and asking me about my trip, she led me outside to catch a cab to her house on N Street. Being in our nation's capital, whizzing through the streets in a taxi, was unbelievable. It only took a few minutes to reach her house. It was a two-story red brick building with a basement on a tree-lined street. Then I was inside meeting the family members who happened to be home at that time. The two youngest, Ruby, who was the baby, and Sterling, who was the youngest boy, were both toddlers. The ones who were in school started to arrive home. Gloria was about seven years old; Kinchen, I think, was around ten; and

Cousin Mary's son Leroy.

Cousin George Faison and Lloyd, Leroy's brother on N Street
in northwest Washington, D.C.

Elnora was thirteen. The two older boys, Leroy and Lloyd, both worked. Georgia, the oldest girl, lived in Newark, New Jersey, and worked as a stenographer. Cousin Kinch, her husband, was a chef in a restaurant near Pennsylvania Avenue where the bigwigs in government ate. The family members also included Cousin George and Cousin Grant, Cousin Mary's brothers. Everybody made me feel right at home. The rooms were old-fashioned and comfortable. Coal furnaces heated the living and dining rooms.

When Elnora came home from school, she asked if I'd like to go to the market with her. That was her after-school job. Cousin Mary instructed her on what to buy and how much. I don't know how long she'd been shopping for her mother, but she was an expert at it. That's how I was introduced to the O Street Market.

It was a large rambling place with a roof and cement floors, and the sides were either open or had lots of windows. Stalls were everywhere. There were vegetables fresh from the country, meats, fish, baked goods, and fruit—everything it seemed. Elnora went from stall to stall, looking at and feeling whatever she was supposed to buy, always some kind of greens, usually kale or cabbage, then the meats. When she was finished, we each had a large shopping bag full and several more packages. That was just for one meal.

We walked the several blocks to and from the market. Cousin Mary cooked dinner. Leroy and Lloyd came in from work. I had met Lloyd earlier, when he had come down to North Carolina to visit with Willie. I liked them both, but Leroy and I hit it off right away. It was as if we had always known each other. When he talked, he would look straight at me. He'd speak plainly and would incorporate a few gestures at the same time. While Cousin Mary cooked dinner and Elnora did chores, he sat in the dining room by the fire with me. We got acquainted. I told him about home and school. He told me about his job at the Treasury Department. He had also taken classes at some point in time. Sterling was right there, talking and wrestling with Ruby.

When the evening paper came, Leroy and Elnora spread it out on the table to see what movies were playing and where. They asked me if I'd like to go to the theater after dinner. "The what?" I asked them. They formed the word *theater* again and pointed to the ads in the paper. I got it; they called the movies the "theater." Down home, it was called the movies or a "picture show." I'd always associated theater with stage plays and live people. I said, "Okay, you mean the movies?"

"Theater," they both repeated, as I looked them in the eye. To me, it was still the movies and I wasn't about to go all-proper and start calling a movie a theater. I compromised and said, "Well, whatever, you all can say theater." They laughed, and it was settled.

Dinners were delicious. Cousin Mary cooked like down-home people—lots of good greens, pork, fried chicken, cornbread, etc. Elnora and I did the dishes, with Leroy pitching in to help tidy the dining room. Cousin Kinch had come in from work, and he and Cousin Mary sat by the fire talking. They called the three of us over and gave us fifty cents each for the movies; I was like one of theirs. Wrapping up good and warm, we set out to go to the theater. There were three moviehouses in the neighborhood, the Raphael, the Broadway, and another one. It was on Seventh Street in a rough part of town. They didn't go there. It only cost thirty-five cents to go in, so we had extra for popcorn and candy. Leroy bought the tickets and found good seats and went back for our treats. What fun we had!

Cousin Mary hadn't forgotten her promise to see about my hearing. She made an early morning appointment for me to be examined at the D.C. Ear, Eye, Nose, and Throat Hospital. As usual, I was scared to pieces. At the doctor's office, they were all nice and gentle with me, but that didn't keep me from almost having a heart attack when I had to put on a white gown and lie down on a white table where a huge black machine on the ceiling started descending toward me. I thought I'd be squashed for sure, but it stopped just a few inches away. I was turned this way and that way, while little red lights winked and blinked. That part was finally over, and then there were needles and blood tests. I was soon allowed to dress and go back to Cousin Mary. They told her the x-rays showed there was nothing to be gained by surgery. My inner ear structure was normal. They'd send the blood test results by mail or call.

On the way out, a couple of ladies wearing gray dresses and scarves draped over their heads wanted to talk with us. (I later learned that they were Gray Ladies, Red Cross volunteers who worked in hospitals.) They wanted to know if I could read and write or communicate with people, and if so, they said they could get me on right there at the hospital working as a maid. At first Cousin Mary couldn't even say anything. She just stared at the women. Then she did let loose on those ladies. She told them in no uncertain terms that I was her cousin Ben's daughter from North Carolina and had just graduated from a fine school and didn't need to be a maid for anybody. She also told them that if I needed a job, she'd see that I was given a government job, in an office at a desk, like theirs. Grabbing my hand, she pulled me along after her. I looked back at the two women sitting there with open mouths.

I think Cousin Mary had hoped to be able to send me back to my folks with my hearing fully restored, and she was disappointed that that couldn't be. But the Gray Ladies had given her an idea—she could help me get a good job. She lost no time in pursuing this effort. An appointment was made for me to see someone else on New York Avenue the following morning, supposedly to see about a hearing aid.

We were up and out early that morning. I learned all about catching streetcars and city buses. I liked the streetcars the best. The fare was ten cents a ride in any direction as far as that car went. The buses were five cents and some times ten.

I was given applications to fill out and notified as to where and when the next civil service exam would be given. The days flew by. I was on the streets with Cousin Mary during the day and with Leroy and Elnora at night. We'd either go to a movie or just walk around the neighborhood. I was tested for a hearing aid. None helped me much, but Cousin Mary put in for a hearing aid company to buy me one anyway. She'd make them do something. It was like I'd found a second home and family.

The notice came for me to report to a government building on Seventh Street in which civil service exams were given.
It wasn't far from Cousin Mary's, but the time was very early—
7:30 a.m. Of course, Cousin Mary had me there on the dot. I
walked into a huge room with rows of school-type desks. I was
given sheets of papers and pencils. Then, I was led to a desk
in the very first row right under the watchful eye of the person giving the test. Pointing to a big clock on the wall, she told
me how much time I had to do the test papers. Nothing was
permitted on the desk except those papers and pencils. I was
taking the test for keypunch operator, something I had never
even heard of before that time. I looked closely at the papers.
My hands were shaking, and my mind was a total blank. Well,
I couldn't let Cousin Mary down since I was her Cousin Ben's
daughter, and with all the walking she'd done on my behalf.
So I did what I always do in a crisis, shut my eyes and asked
my Lord for his help. Some of the questions and math problems were easy; however, there were some I found hard to
believe anyone knew, regardless of whether they were hearing or nonhearing. We only had a certain amount of time to
finish and to hand over the papers to one of several attendants
who were watching us. I did the problems I was sure of but
didn't waste much time on the others. I put down what I
thought most likely to be the correct answer. I finished ahead
of time and put my name, address, and so on on the papers,
along with the time it had taken me to finish. It was less than
an hour. Then I said a silent prayer that I had at least made a
passing mark, and I headed downstairs to try to find my way
back to Cousin Mary's house. At the bottom of the stairs stood
Leroy waiting for me. I was giddy with relief.

"Boy, am I glad to see you," I said.

"Ma sent me, so you wouldn't get lost. Come on."

It was cold, with a light rain falling. We decided to walk the few blocks to N Street. Leroy was tall and took long steps, but I had no trouble keeping up with him. I was a fast walker like my pop. However, my hands and nose were freezing. I put one hand in Leroy's overcoat pocket, the other inside my coat; my nose, I couldn't do anything about.

It wasn't too long before we were back in Cousin Mary's warm dining room. "How did it go?" she asked me.

"I don't know, I was scared at first, but I got all right and finished before my time was up."

"Good!" Cousin Mary beamed. "I knew you could do it." I wasn't so sure, as there'd been some hard problems and questions on those sheets of paper. However, much to my surprise, a letter arrived a day or so later that was addressed to me, saying I had passed the test; in fact, I scored 96. There were no openings for keypunch operators at the time, and I was instructed to return for another test, naming the date and time. I thought, "Oh boy, another hour of torture." I was ready to forget the whole thing and go back to Richmond and then on home. Christmas was getting closer. Again, I decided, I couldn't let my Cousin Mary down, so I went back at the appointed time. It was a repeat of the first, only I took the test for junior clerk. It was a little harder this time. I scored 94 and was told they would notify me as soon as I was appointed to a position.

Cousin Mary was a happy woman. Everyone who came to her house heard about her Cousin Ben's little girl, and that she already knew I could do it, which was more than I could say for myself. A girl who lived there asked if I had finished high school. She said she didn't see a class ring. "She don't need no class ring," my cousin said. "Her ring is in her head." Actually I had a class pin, but I seldom wore it. I decided to go on home so I could be there for Christmas.

Back in Richmond, Eunice was busy shopping and getting ready for our trip home. Her husband, R. C., had to get paid and then get leave. We finally got to the railroad station. It was crowded with servicemen trying to get home or make it back to some base to be shipped out for Europe or the Pacific. We could only get two tickets on the train, so R. C. said for me and Eunice to take them and he'd catch a later train or bus. The problem was his clothes had already been packed in the same bag with Eunice's. She had to open the bag and unpack his longjohn underwear and other clothes. This was done with people all around us, but nobody seemed to care.

Getting on the train was a hard job. The crowd pushed and shoved, trying to make sure they'd have seats. The servicemen had been let on first. It was patriotic to make sure they had the best of everything, because they were fighting for our country in two different places, Japan and Germany. Once on the train we managed to find seats and had fun flirting with the guys all the way home. We got there in time to help with the baking and decorating for Christmas.

Maxine was a cute little two-year-old by this time. It sure did liven things up to have a baby in the house for Santa Claus to visit. She wanted a soda for her Christmas, so Christmas Eve night, her dad brought her a whole case of sodas. Then Eunice started celebrating by getting high on Christmas spirits. R. C. had brought Eunice a lovely blue coat with a silver fox collar and black velvet spike heel sandals. When Frank suggested a ride on his motorcycle, Effie, my sister put on her pretty coat and shoes, hopped on the back, and away they roared. Poor Mama did what she always did when any of the family was absent and she was worried. She walked our long porch from one end to the other and prayed. I went out to keep her company. It was a bright, clear moonlit night, and very cold. Every so often she'd stop and listen and tell me where she heard them at. They would roar down the highway toward the creek, then come by again heading north toward town. She'd walk until she heard them again. At long last her face brightened, and she said they'd slowed down for the turn in on our road. Sure enough, it was only a little while before we could see the small headlight flashing through the trees, and then it was in the yard. I guess the icy cold December air must have cleared their heads. On Christmas morning it was fun to see Maxine open her gifts, all wide-eyed and wondering as only a child can be at the magic of that wonderful night and day.

After the holidays, things settled back to normal. Again, I was following my favorite path through the woods to Gladys's house. The happy hours were spent discussing the guys we were most interested in. She knew the most guys—Peanut, Elroy, his brother, and another guy named Sam. The ones I liked best were the ones I'd gone to school with or the ones already in the service. We had fun discussing her guys and walking the road with what was left of our gang.

One Sunday after Sunday school, all of us started out walking, heading no place in particular. We soon found ourselves on the Katy Ford Road. "Let's walk to the Katy Ford," someone said. We all agreed. This was a place where the creek crossed the road under an old wooden bridge. Some white woman named Katy and her baby had died there. I've forgotten exactly what happened, but it was a tragedy, and the place looked spooky. There were no houses close by, just swamps, cypress, and live oaks with lots of Spanish moss hanging down. The water ran under the bridge, gurgling, and some people said they'd sometimes hear a baby crying. Well, that was our destination. Upon reaching it, the boys tried to scare us girls by pretending they saw or heard something. We were about ready to turn back, when someone noticed a wagon trail leading into the swamp. Then, suddenly, it was, "Let's follow this trail and see where it goes."

The girls protested because we only had on shoes and socks and our feet would get wet.

"No problem," the boys assured us. "We'll tote you gals across."

Gladys looked at me and I looked at her, "Well?" The other girls, Ruth Mae, Doris, Beck, Otelia, Dot, and Lib, all said they'd rather do whatever we did. The boys weren't waiting for any such decision, they were busy taking off their shoes and socks, tying the laces together, and rolling up their pants legs. That done, each one grabbed the nearest girl, told her to get on his back, and handed her his shoes to hang on to. We were ferried across until all were on dry, or at least solid, ground. Shoes and socks were put back on. This was in January on a cold Sunday. Our mothers would have had a hissy fit if they were where they had been able to see their offspring. We proceeded on our way, with absolutely no idea where we would come out of the woods. At long last, the woods thinned out, and the kids said they heard somebody. Trying to be quiet, we eased up to the edge of the trees, and lo and behold, we'd come upon a funeral being held in a field near the woods. Then we spotted a mule and cart hitched to a tree. The mule was dozing while the funeral was going on with prayers and singing. "That's Mr. John David's mule," someone said. "Yes, and there he is with Cousin Archie, Bob and Dot's grandfather."

The next idea was to hitch a ride home. We were in Boney Town, a community about five miles from Iron Mine, where we lived. Keeping quiet, so as not to attract attention, we went to the cart. There was a board across the front. Gladys and I were given this seat, and the rest sat on the floor and sides of the cart while some of the boys sat across the back with legs dangling, ready to ride. That's what Cousin Archie and Mr. John David found wait-

ing for them when they got back. Those were some surprised
men when they returned. Mr. John David thought it funny to find
his cart packed with kids. Cousin Archie did not find it amusing
at all. He declared he wasn't riding with them young'uns, he'd
rather walk back across the Katy Ford. Gladys and I squeezed
together to make room for him on the seat of honor we shared.
He sat down, took off his socks and shoes, rolled up his pants,
found a long stick, and entered the swamp where we came out,
to walk in peace. Mr. John David climbed up to sit on the board
with us and drive his mule—only the mule wouldn't budge at
first. When he did try to move, he strained and pulled to get the
cart started. Some of our gallant males got off and pushed from
the back to help the poor mule get a start. I felt sorry for that
mule. He didn't look any too robust to start with, but he strained
and pulled us over cornfields covered with stubble and rutted dirt
roads. Finally we reached Highway 41, which was paved. The
mule was so happy to find its burden easier to pull on a smooth,
hard, surface that he immediately broke into a trot. We jogged
along heading toward the west and home, when all of a sudden
there was a loud crack and Gladys and I found ourselves sitting
on the floor among the rest of the children. Oh, the shrieks and
laugher that this mishap brought on. Another board was found,
and we resumed our journey, but not for long. A chain on the
mule's harness was next to go. This took longer to repair, as Mr.
John David had to find a piece of wire to hold the broken chain
together. While this was going on, two girl friends passed by
riding in a nice car with some older guys I didn't know. They were
horrified to see me riding down Highway 41 in a mule and cart
on a Sunday evening. They stopped and beckoned for me to ride
with them. All the kids stopped laughing and turned their eyes
on me. I was having so much fun I wasn't about to leave. I
thanked them but said I'd finish out the ride I was already on.

They argued for a while, but finally moved on. Everybody started grinning again and waved the car on.

By this time the chain was repaired and again the mule resumed its task of getting a carload of young'uns home. The sun was fixing to go down, and the January air was cool and nippy. The mule must have smelled home, for he broke into another trot. Nothing broke this time, and it wasn't long before we started jumping off at our various homes.

# 2

# The Start of My Big City Life

*Adieu! Adieu! Thy plaintive anthem fades*
*. . . and now 'tis buried deep*
*In the next valley glades.*

John Keats,
"Ode to a Nightingale"

I DIDN'T know it then, but this would be the last time some of this crowd would ramble about and have fun together. We were fast approaching the time our paths would diverge and we would begin to travel in different directions. Only a day or so later I received a long white envelope from the U.S. Government, Civil Service, Washington, D.C. I was to report to a specific building on January 18. That would be the next Monday. I would be leaving home on Sunday. I could see that Mama was proud of what I was doing, although she'd never told me she wanted me to go out and work at a job far away from home. The choice was mine. I don't know how the rest of the family felt. Sam asked me once why I wanted to go to Washington, and he assured me I was going to perish and come back nothing but skin and bones. Papa as usual, was against my going anywhere, and he told Mama I just wanted to go there to ramble up and down the streets like I did in Iron Mine, and then he'd bring out his favorite saying: "She's got no more business there than a pig has with a Bible." When I tried to picture one of Papa's fat curly-tailed pigs sitting up reading a Bible, it struck me as funny indeed and I'd giggle. I told Mama to tell him I didn't want to ramble in Washington. I was going to work. The answer to that was, "Oh pshaw, she don't have to go to work. She has a home."

I spent the week packing my footlocker with as many clothes as I could and sorting out family and school pictures and books that I wanted to carry, along with the gifts the gang had given me for my birthday only two short weeks before. It still didn't seem quite real that I was leaving home, and this time it was not for school, but clean out of North Carolina. I had just turned eighteen and was an adult and would be responsible for my own food, rent, clothes, and so on.

Gladys wanted to go with me, but her dad said no, she didn't have to go out and work for a living. Mama said I didn't either, but I wanted to be independent and take care of myself. Well, Sunday came around. It was the third Sunday of the month, which was our preaching Sunday. We went to church as usual. I said good-bye to all the gang who were at church. I almost felt like I did when I first went away to school in Raleigh. I also said good-bye to our pastor, Mr. Tim. I'd miss our little white wooden church, Sunday school, and the preaching on third Sundays.

Mama fixed dinner, and we ate. All my things were packed and ready. We'd be leaving for the bus station shortly afterwards. I was catching the afternoon bus so I'd arrive in D.C. early the next morning. Right after dinner, someone arrived at the house with Frank. He'd been riding Effie, his motorcycle, and when rounding a sharp curve on the way home, he had been thrown off the bike, landing in a field with Effie on top of him. His chest had been bruised. Thank the Lord it was no worse, but it was so upsetting that I didn't want to leave. After putting Frank to bed and looking at his chest, Mama said it didn't look all that bad and for me to go on as planned. I didn't want to leave my brother Frank there hurting, but she said they would send for the doctor to come see about him. House calls by doctors were made willingly in those days. My trunk was put in the truck and I was soon on my way to the bus station with Papa, Mama, and little Maxine. Eunice was back in Richmond. Sam declined to see me off this time.

Papa bought my ticket and checked my baggage, and we sat in the truck waiting for the bus to roll in. When it did, I felt like I was in a dream and this wasn't me fixing to get on a Greyhound bus and ride hundreds of miles from home to start a new life on my own. No longer were there teachers or a housemother or a whole building full of kids to play with, fuss with, or share with. Silently Papa lifted my bags and small trunk from the truck, and attached tags, without looking at me. I hugged Mama hard and little Maxine, then turned to Papa. He handed me my ticket and only then looked at me. His eyes were sad, and I almost told him to put my things back in the truck, that I wasn't going no place, but he sort of gave me a little push toward the bus driver waiting by the open door. I hastily kissed his cheek, saying "Bye Papa," and stumbled up the bus steps, found a seat, and sat down. The bus started up. I settled in my seat, reading until it started darkening up. Then I just looked out the window. The route was familiar, the same highway I'd been traveling all these years, going to and from school. I realized we'd be passing through Raleigh on Highway 70. I sat alert, keeping my eyes open for the first sight of my old school. It wasn't long. We rounded the curve I'd watched so often from my classroom, and there it was outlined against the early evening dusk. I saw the boys' dorms and then the administration building. Next I saw the dining hall, and then there it was, my dorm, with all the windows lit up. I could imagine the girls gathered in little groups near a radiator, gossiping and sharing whatever food any of them had managed to smuggle in from the kitchen. It was Sunday, so there'd be extra goodies. I felt so lonely for my old gang and the life I used to have. I watched it through the water in my eyes until the bus rounded another curve and I could see it no longer.

We reached Richmond sometime that night and had to change over to another bus. This one was crowded, and I had to sit in a corner on the last seat in the back. I didn't mind too much. Some people were standing in the aisle or sitting on suitcases. The bus dimmed its lights inside so people could sleep, and it hummed along the highway. I dozed in my corner but woke up when the bus stopped and whoever was sitting next to me got off. Another person immediately took the space and was rude, pushing and shoving. I huddled as far away as I could and tried to go to sleep, but I smelled a terrible odor. Turning my head to see what was nearby, it was my new seatmate, a ratty-looking man with snaggly teeth trying to talk to me, with a horrible smell of garlic, fish, and whatever he'd been eating blowing directly in my face. I turned to the window again. He jabbed me with his elbow, trying to get me to turn around and talk. I had a small case with me on the floor. I picked it up and stood it upright in my lap and hid my face behind it. The smell kept coming, so I knew his mouth must be open. The bus stopped all of a sudden, and when I peeped around my bag I saw the bus driver standing there talking to the man. After that he quieted down and left me alone. But I could still smell him. Sleep wouldn't come anymore, so I thought about home and my dear family.

Usually when I traveled, I made friends somewhere along the way. If anyone looked at me and smiled I was quick to smile back. If they spoke, I'd tell them I was deaf. They'd nod and find paper and pencil to write whatever they wanted to say. Some preferred to talk and make gestures. That was okay too. However, this time I didn't try to make any friends. I had a lot on my mind. Did I really want this? To leave the South that had always been my home, along with the people I knew and loved? I'd be living and working among strangers, hearing strangers at that. I knew how hurtful some of them could be. Would I be able to work? I'd had no college education. I thought of all the pros and cons. Finally my mind tired of it all, and I decided to let it rest and just keep going until I saw how things would turn out. My adventurous spirit returned, and I felt better.

It had begun to get light outside, and my smelly seatmate had gotten off sometime during the night. I started seeing things I recognized along the way, and I knew we were nearing Washington. Preparing to get off, I put on my coat and the new brown felt hat I'd gotten for fall. So here I was arriving in the nation's capital, ready to set out on a new life and a new adventure. It wasn't long in coming. Not only was my cousin nowhere to be seen this time, but it was pouring rain and cold.

After making sure I didn't see anybody even slightly resembling anyone I knew, I sat down to wait and think about what I could do. After no one came through the door looking for me, I decided the only thing I could do was look for them. That meant taking a taxi to the house on N Street. I buttoned up my coat, pulled my hat to what I hoped was a smart angle, and ventured out on New York Avenue, like I'd been doing this for years. Cars and taxis whizzed by, some stopping to pick up or let out passengers. None stopped for me. I held up my fingers like I'd seen others do. They still whizzed by and stopped for someone else, while I got wetter by the minute. I stood my ground wet and frozen. My smart brown hat brim hanging so low all I could see were tires and the bottoms of car doors. Finally I saw tires stop in front of me and a door open. Thank you, Lord! I leaped directly in the back seat and fell smack dab in a haughty-looking white woman's lap. I was in and not getting back out. "Scuse me, scuse me," I said, raising myself up enough for her to get out. I think she thought she'd tangled with a nut. No matter, I settled back on those cushions waiting for the cab to start up and deliver me to Cousin Mary's door. When it didn't start, I lifted my dripping hat brim to see what was wrong with the driver. He had turned around with his chin propped in his hands looking at me. We stared at each other until it hit me that I hadn't even told the man where I wanted to go. "Oh my goodness, I'm sorry," I said, and I gave him the address. He looked a little longer, then kind of smiled, turned around, and started his car. I guess he had decided I wasn't dangerous. Thus, my big city life began.

# 3

# A New Job

WELL, my Cousin Mary hadn't forgotten me. She had had an important appointment and had asked Lloyd to pick me up. He said he went, but didn't see me anyplace and thought I probably hadn't come or would be on a later bus, so he left, intending to check back by. Oh, well, I'd found my way.

Now things really got down to business. I was told to go to first one big government building down on Constitution Avenue, then another, always filling out more forms. I noticed that each place I went, there would be several black women there doing the same thing. Finally, we were in the same place having pictures made for identification. When it was my turn to get before that huge black machine and look at a little red light, I couldn't make up my mind whether to smile or look cool and dignified. I looked neither. The camera caught me just as one side of my mouth started up, so it was lopsided, as were my glasses. It was an amazingly lopsided picture, but they sealed it in a case with a black ribbon attached to be worn around my neck as long as I was inside

or on the grounds of the building I'd been assigned to work in.
Then on to another building. My legs, already short, felt like
they'd worn down to a nub. Next stop was across the street. We
reached this by a walkway high over the street. The room looked
more like a lounge, decorated with plants, pictures, and flags.
Here we met with a couple of naval officers, who sported lots of
gold braids. We learned we'd be working at the Navy Annex in
Arlington, Virginia, across the Potomac River. I think they'd been
told about me, for they gave me a thick set of papers to read while
they lectured the rest of the group about the nature of our work.
It was very confidential and not to be discussed outside the office, and there were other rules and regulations.

After checking to see if I had read and understood everything
or if I had any questions to ask (I was too much in awe to ask
questions), they proceeded to swear us in with a Bible and with
our right hands raised. After we had sworn never to do anything
to undermine or to overthrow our government, they shook hands
with us and wished us good luck, and we were on our way. That
being settled, an aide went with us to show how to get over to
Arlington. There was a bus terminal on Pennsylvania Avenue
where we could get a bus to Virginia.

Through all of this, my dear Cousin Mary had been right there
with me. However, on reaching the Navy Annex, she was told
she'd have to return on the same bus. No one without an ID tag
could go through those gates. A tall fence topped with barbed
wire surrounded the place. I saw only two gates, each guarded by
two well-armed marines. Guns were mounted on top of the building. Cousin Mary asked the other women in the group if some
of them would look out for me and see that I got back over to
D.C. okay. They assured her that they would. She got back on
the bus. They were all older women, but they became my friends
from that day on. There was Marie, or Howard, rather. All used

last names: Mills, Mitchell, Quarles, Murphy, and Raymond. These would be among my best friends for the years I spent there and afterward.

We were shown the office we would be working in, and introduced to the daytime staff. It was wartime, and more people were needed to keep up with the paperwork. Therefore, they were starting a four-to-twelve shift. Next, we were guided to the cafeterias located on the ground floor. There we got in line and ordered lunch. This was new to me. At home a waitress took your order and brought it to the table. Here it was more like an assembly line—take a tray, silverware, and napkins, pick out a salad if you wanted one, and next, desserts. Then, women in white uniforms would serve our choice of two vegetables and whatever meat or soup we wanted and then, bread, butter, milk, tea, or whatever. Finally we came to the cashier. A meal of two vegetables, meat, bread and butter, and a beverage was usually thirty-five cents. Desserts were extra. I didn't know what to order because I didn't even recognize some of the food. I did know fried oysters, so that's what I selected, along with bread and iced tea.

We found a table and started getting to know each other. Mills, I liked at once. She was a friendly down-to-earth person. She'd just married for the second time and had two young daughters, nine and eleven. Howard, also from North Carolina, was still with her first husband and had a grown son. I liked her too. She was plump and pretty with shiny black eyes and lots of jokes. The others were nice, but I didn't really get to know them that day. Lunch over, we found our way back to the third floor, where our boss, Mr. Gaskins, told us to check in promptly at four o'clock the following day. Then it was outside and to the gate and the guardhouse, where we had to show our ID tags to get out and wait for the bus back to D.C. Not knowing just which streetcar to catch, we pooled and got a taxi. I was first out. The rest lived farther up in some of the better parts of town or at least they were at that time—near Meridian Hill, now Martin Luther King Park. That was the big place where black night clubs, restaurants, and other places of entertainment were located. People who lived on any of the streets, such as Florida Avenue, Blair Road , Fairmont, and others had it good. N Street was mixed and middle class.

Cousin Mary was waiting to hear how my day went after she left me. I had to relate everything that happened, even to coming out to go home and finding it snowing. She smiled and beamed through it all, until I told what I'd had for lunch. She rolled her eyes in distaste. I'll fix you a lunch tomorrow, and that she did! The next day, she and I left her house for Pennsylvania Avenue promptly at 3 p.m. On boarding the streetcar on Eleventh Street, there were Mills and a couple more girls I'd met the previous day. The rest were waiting for the Arlington bus. When we got there, Cousin Mary handed me the brown paper bag she'd been carrying, told me good-bye, and headed back home to cook dinner for her family.

I was still in a state of disbelief that this was really *me*, on a bus heading for a real government job, without any of my family or school people. I loved everything about it, passing so many of the places I'd only read about before—the Lincoln Memorial, the Washington Monument, the Treasury Department, the Department of Agriculture, then on across the Potomac, and past the cherry trees and the tidal basin, and we passed right underneath the Pentagon. My eyes must have been as big as saucers. When I looked at my future coworkers to see how they took all these wonders, they were watching me and smiling—nice friendly smiles though, so I didn't mind. The bus dropped us off right in front of the marine guards. The girls motioned for me to follow them and show my ID tag to the guards. I was sure they would laugh when they saw mine, but there was only a glance at my tag, then my face. Nothing was said, and those scary-looking guns didn't come out, so we passed on. Inside, we passed through the lobby where blind people ran concession stands, selling candy, snacks, and newspapers. Being as we were all new, we had to search for an elevator to take us to the third floor. Then, there was another search for the Muster Roll Department, where we'd be working. We found it with a few minutes to spare.

The day force was checking out as we were checking in. Someone showed us where to hang our coats, but we could keep our bags in our desks. Each of us was assigned a desk after being introduced to our bosses and the rest of the night force who had been working there for a while. Mr. Gaskins was boss of this department, and Miss Coates was our supervisor. While Miss Coates gathered the new girls in a group and explained how things were done, Mr. Gaskins took me in hand and led me to my desk. He brought some reports, or muster rolls as they were called, and showed me how to check the current roll against the one from the prior month, and how to write letters for the typists to type up, if necessary. It only took me a few minutes to catch on. I wasn't uncomfortable with him at all. He looked like my brother Frank—about the same age, with the same build and coloring. Was I ever a happy little country gal. This was a piece of cake. My next thrill was when he brought me a binder of a ship's muster rolls and told me to check them and then file them away again, in the proper order. All of the desks were large, olive green steel with heavy, deep drawers. I checked away.

Six o'clock was dinnertime. Mills and Howard came for me to go to dinner. Taking Cousin Mary's brown bag out of the drawer, I followed them. A few more also carried bags, but not as large as mine. I only had to buy a beverage as my cousin had instructed me to do. One of the other girls who had brought lunch told me to find a table I liked and said she would bring me my drink. About four or five of us sat at a table. When I opened my bag to see what Cousin Mary had packed and laid it out on the table, all eyes were upon me. I had about a half of a chicken, ham, bread, fruit (two or three pieces), and a huge hunk of pound cake. One girl said, "My, are you going to eat all of that?"

"I guess," I said. It was a typical Cousin Mary lunch.

"Well, no wonder you are so nice and plump," she said.

A nice way to tell me I was fat, I thought. I said nothing but enjoyed my lunch. We had an hour off for lunch and then it was back to the third floor. I enjoyed the work. To me it was very interesting to see the names of all the boys and navy men, where they were, and what they did. I also found it awesome to know I had been trusted with this information, and I understood why we had to be fingerprinted and photographed. Signs all over the place showed Uncle Sam with a finger to his lips, saying "Shh, the slip of a lip can sink a ship." At ten o'clock, a couple of girls came around collecting change for snacks down on the first floor. After my big lunch, I only wanted a soda and candy. The soda was five cents a cup. A candy bar of any kind was five or ten cents. Sandwiches were also ten cents—ham and cheese, roast beef, and so on. We had a short break, during which time we visited each other's desks, wrote letters, or read a little. Then at eleven thirty we would tidy our desks, turn any letters we had to write over to the typist to be typed up, then sign out promptly at twelve o'clock.

Not many people worked at night. A couple of buses waited at the gate to transport us back to D.C. I traveled with the same group I came in with. Again the scenery was to be marveled at—the Washington skyline at night from the Virginia side of the river: the Capital Dome, the Washington Monument, the eerie-looking blue light shining on and around the statue of Lincoln, and the

Potomac River, reflecting the lights from the bridges spanning the river. Just to think I was in the same town as the president and Mrs. Roosevelt. One year Mrs. Roosevelt had visited Wallace during strawberry season. There had been a festival, and somehow she'd gotten on top of a boxcar sitting on the railroad tracks and danced a jig with a flowered dress and hat on. How the people loved her. She, our governor Clyde Hoey, and his wife had been the guests of Dr. and Mrs. Robinson, so I felt like I knew her. My pop swore by Roosevelt and how much he was doing for everybody, and bought up anything he saw on sale pertaining to our president. He purchased buttons, posters, and even canned Brunswick stew because he heard Roosevelt liked it. Now he was trying to beat the enemy to protect our country, and I was doing my bit to help—a part of all this, not a big part, but here I was, and so proud of it.

When we reached Pennsylvania Avenue, you might have known, there stood Leroy, waiting for me in the cold. His mom sure didn't mean for me to get lost. The girls looked at me with teasing grins and raised eyebrows when Leroy came forward and walked beside me. Well, mercy do, they thought he was my boyfriend. "Hey," I said, "This is my Cousin Mary's son Leroy." They knew her all right. I introduced them all, and we headed for the Eleventh Street car stop. All seemed to be going in the same direction.

Leroy and I were first to get off. It was a two-block walk to the house. As usual, Cousin Mary was up by the heater waiting to hear how everything went. After taking off my coat and hat, I couldn't wait to get started. She was pleased to hear how I got along with everyone and could do the work as required, and laughed when told what they said about my lunch. "I want you to have plenty of good food. You can't work on an empty stomach." I was told. She also said a lot of women up there spent

money on fancy clothes and hairdo's and starved. It was agreed
Leroy would meet me at Eleventh and N instead of Pennsylvania
Avenue since I had lots of company on the streetcar. They all rode
much farther down. She also said for me to sleep as late as I
wanted to since I worked at night. Next morning I tried, but I
was too used to the 6 a.m. rising bell at school and farm life, which
also started with sun-up or before. So, I only stayed in bed until
all were off to school and work, then went downstairs to join
Cousin Mary and her two youngest, Ruby and Sterling. After a
smile and a cheerful good morning, she asked me if I'd mind
running to the store for her so we could have some breakfast.

"No m'am," I said, "which one?" There were two close by.
One was in the middle of our block and was run by an elderly
white (Jewish, I think) couple. The other one was on the corner
of Ninth and N Street. "Either one." She gave me a list of what
she wanted to buy—hard rolls, pork sausage, eggs, and juice—
and some change. The old couple knew me very well by now
from seeing me come in previously with Cousin Mary's children.
I felt at home. After filling the order and paying for the items, I
returned to the house and played with the kids while Cousin
Mary fixed our breakfast. It was delicious, and I loved those hard
rolls. I've never had them outside of D.C. They were about the
size of a medium hamburger roll, brown and crusty outside, soft
and tender within, and not gummy or mushy. Tea was the morning drink here, served piping hot with sugar and lemon. After
breakfast, we talked and talked. It was wonderful to catch up on
the years I hadn't known her. I was given a rundown of Papa's
family tree and all the aunts, uncles, cousins, and others I'd never
heard of. Some lived in different parts of North Carolina, some
were over in Baltimore, and others were at home. She went back
and traced grands and great-grands, their children and how each
was related to the other. Before I knew it, it was time for me to

get dressed and catch the streetcar to Pennsylvania Avenue so I'd be there when the Arlington bus came in. It was too late to fix a bag lunch. We decided that I would buy lunch today. Just as well. Those guards at the gate had to open every bag or box passing there.

And so, a new and very different lifestyle started for me, one that I'd never dreamed of. However, once I was in bed and ready to go to sleep, pictures of home and school rose up before me. I was either back at the school on Garner Road with my old crowd or at home, telling all about my new life, the job, people I'd met, places I'd been to, and most of all Cousin Mary and her family. So, things settled into a daily routine. By now I'd learned the neighborhood streets fairly well and could catch the streetcar at Eleventh and N, and then the Arlington bus at Pennsylvania Avenue on my own, check in at four o'clock, and catch a bus back to D.C. at midnight.

I was happy and life was good, especially when my first payday rolled around, and I was handed my check in a brown envelope. I'd never had that much money at one time in my life. Now, I could start doing what I'd dreamed of doing for so long—send Mama and Papa money and buy something for Sam. After putting my paycheck in my handbag, I put it in the bottom drawer of my desk and pushed it shut. At quitting time, when I reached down to open the drawer, it was locked! Try as I might, it wouldn't open and no key anywhere. One of the girls called Mr. Gaskins. He came over and tried, but no go. People were checking out, and there I was with no purse, not even for carfare home. Finally Mr. Gaskins somehow got it open. I breathed a sigh of relief. Now I had change to pay busfare home, and I also had my first real paycheck. I could have hugged Mr. Gaskin's neck but didn't dare. At home, that would have been the natural thing to do, but I didn't know these people well enough to have any idea

whether they'd say, "Look at that little fast thing," or what. I just
thanked him and let it go.

The next day, Cousin Mary took me to a branch bank just
around the corner on Ninth Street and showed me how to get my
check cashed. I had made seventy-two dollars. That was consid-
ered good money in the days when the hourly pay for housework
was thirty-five cents an hour, or at the most, fifty-cents. The
household duties included cleaning the house, doing laundry,
light cooking, and sometimes tending a kid or two on the side.
Farm work paid even less. So you can see, I was really proud of
that check. Since all of Cousin Mary's working children gave her
money for room and board, I did the same, and then I sent some
money to Mama and Papa. It wasn't time for the crops yet, and I
knew they could use the money.

My life sailed on and was very different from campus life. I
was still unable to sleep very late. My years of farm life and school
days were still very much a part of me. I was usually home by
twelve-thirty if the buses and streetcars were running on time.
Cousin Mary was always still waiting up and ready to listen to my
daily happenings after I'd had a light supper. The workers and
schoolchildren had gone when I got up. Then I would run to one
or the other of the neighborhood grocery stores to get our breakfast which was usually the same things, pork sausage, eggs, hard
rolls, and sometimes grapefruit. It was fun playing with Sterling
and Ruby while breakfast cooked. Sterling kept you laughing.
Ruby was the baby and still sucked her thumb.

When breakfast was over and the dishes washed, Cousin Mary
would change her seat by the furnace for a chair in front of her
living room window facing the street. It was a bow window, one
on each side, so she had a good view in both directions without
having to stick her head out. She must have been doing this for
a good while because most of the people who passed seemed to

know her and stopped to chat. After they passed on, she'd tell me who the people were and where they lived. Most of them lived on Eleventh Street or around the corner on Tenth or Ninth and sometimes, further away. I'd also get a rundown on their lives. Sometimes I'd get dressed and ramble around. I had learned my way around in downtown Washington quite well. My favorite places were the five-and-tens, such as Murphy's, Kress, and others. I also found little old shops that sold old books and other odds and ends, and a Fanny Farmer chocolate shop. All of my exploring was done from N Street on down to Pennsylvania Avenue. I never ventured toward uptown. That was where the nightclubs and other places of entertainment were located. I'd be back home and ready to leave for work by three o'clock. Work was going fine. By now I knew everyone on the night force and had even made friends with a few who worked the day shift. Raymond had the desk next to mine; the next desk was Mills's. She had just remarried and changed her last name to Jones. She had married the first time at a young age and moved to Brooklyn to live with her husband. They'd had two little girls, and her husband had gotten a job on a train as a porter. The train run was between New York and California. That left little time for his family. All of the responsibility of raising the children was on his young wife. Finally, she took her babies and moved back to D.C. with her mother, divorced the porter, and started a new life. Raymond also lived with her parents. I think her husband was in service. She had no children.

My job was so exciting. At times I marveled at how I happened to be in this place doing this work. The Muster Roll Department was a very long room, and the desks were three to a row with about four rows on each end of the room. Mr. Gaskins and Miss Coates, our supervisors, had desks in the center of the room, along with the desks that belonged to the typists. Both sections of desks faced the supervisors. The entire inside walls were shelves on which the filing binders were stored. The outside wall was a long row of windows. These looked out on Arlington National Cemetery, which was just across the street. My desk was the first one in the front row closest to the bosses. Raymond had the middle desk, and Mills, or Jones rather, had the desk by the window. Some of the staff worked at a long table on the far end of the room opening and sorting mail and incoming reports. These reports were filed in the binders on the shelves. Each binder had the name of a ship, naval station, school, or whatever, on the back. Miss Coates assigned to each of us the name of a ship or place to check.

We would locate the particular binder, take it to our desks, and check the current monthly report against the previous month's report. Each man had to be accounted for, including how many were still on board, how many were killed or missing, hospitalized or in the brig, making sure that no one had been left out. We were responsible for writing letters requesting that updates on the whereabouts of the enlisted men be sent in. These letters were taken to a typist to type up and pass on to Miss Coates. This, too, was exciting. I saw many names that were unusual, and that some of the guys in the brig were given only bread and water with a full rationing every other day, plus loss of pay for a period of time. I thought, poor guys. Most of the confinements were for being AWOL, while some were for fighting. If we couldn't find a name we were searching for in Muster Roll, Miss Coates would write us a pass to go to the file room on the floor below us and we could search for the missing man's personal file. These files were kept in heavy orange envelopes and contained everything about him. I say "he" and "him" because although there were women, or WAVES, in the navy at that time, there were none listed onboard the ships and stations that we checked.

Some of the women who worked in the building were part of the women marines, while others were members of the WAVES. They had barracks for them a little farther down the street from the Annex and at another place on the opposite side called Arlington Farms. Sometimes you could look out the window and a bunch of the enlisted women would be drilling. How I loved to watch them stepping in perfect time, stopping, saluting, and pivoting on their heels. I could watch them all night. We could only spend but so much time away from our desks, so it was back to work.

At first, I was assigned easy reports, places here in the United States with only a couple hundred men. That was a piece of cake, and I could do several in one night. Then I started getting more difficult ones, starting with at least a thousand men. I was really excited when I was told to do the *U.S.S. North Carolina*. I felt like they were all my hometown boys. Along with the girls who were hired at the same time I was, I had to attend workshop on the third floor for a few weeks, where we learned more about naval operations. We first studied from books, and then they showed films so that we could learn to recognize different types of naval vessels by their silhouettes on the water—such as battleships, destroyers, aircraft carriers, PT boats, and landing craft. And always, there was a picture of Uncle Sam and his goatee beard telling us to shhh. As you can imagine, I was so awestruck by all of this to-do I didn't need anyone to say shhh. At the end of the program, they made sure I had understood and knew all that I was required to know in order to do my job. I was given a separate test.

# 4

# Cute Boy on the Train

*To that same lot, however mean or high,*
*Toward which Time leads me, and the will of Heaven;*
*All is, if I have grace to use it so,*
*As ever in my great Taskmaster's eye.*

John Milton,
"How Soon Hath Time"

SUNDAY was my only day off, so I felt I could sleep even later than usual. But one Sunday morning, quite early, one of the kids came upstairs and told me I had a male visitor downstairs. Since Sam had always been able to find a bus traveling to wherever I might be, I thought it might be him, but this was February and he'd be in school. I got up, dressed, combed my hair, and headed downstairs, wondering who my visitor could be. Upon reaching the living room, there sat, guess who? None other than my school friend Sonny Davis. He was the first classmate I'd seen since leaving school almost a year ago. How glad I was to see him!

We settled down to sign and catch up on school news and what we'd been doing. At least I signed—he mostly talked, using as few signs as possible. He still hated being deaf and having to use signs. The record player was on and going full blast, as that's the way Cousin Mary's kids liked it. One of them ran in to adjust it, looked at us, and ran back out. In a little while another one marched in and did his bit. They did this until all the younger ones had been in the room. Each time we would get quick, curious looks, and each time Sonny would stop signing and stare back at the children. I couldn't help giggling a little. He was always so uncomfortable with anyone watching him sign. Finally, all of the kids had been in and had their look. We settled back to talk or sign, then the older members found reasons to pass the wide doorway of the living room to go or come through the front door.

"My goodness, how many people live in this house?" he asked me.

"Well, Cousin Mary has seven children, then two of her brothers, her husband, some men who are boarders, two other girls in addition to me, and Cousin Mary herself."

"Whew!" he said. Then he started telling me how Don and Madga had married and had their own apartment and were so happy.

"Great," I said, "I'm glad for them."

"Then be happy for us," he told me, reaching into a bag for a box of chocolates and then a smaller box. He handed me the candy and opened the other box and took out a shiny gold ring with a small, but beautiful, diamond. "This is for you, Mary," he told me. "I have a good job and we can get an apartment right near Don and Madga, and have a good life too."

I looked at the ring, and I looked at Sonny. I felt so bad. He had been my friend for the past two years. We'd had fun in school, passing notes, talking, arguing, and exchanging gifts, but get married now? I just couldn't do it! Here I was just starting out with an exciting and important job, and although I was among hearing people, I was getting along fine, doing my work just as well as the hearing people did. I was even paying my own living expenses and buying a twenty-five-dollar war bond once a month to help the war effort and sending Mama and Papa money each payday. For the first time in my life I felt that I was really managing my life as well as the next person, hearing or nonhearing. I was happy and at peace with God and man.

"Sonny," I said, "I cannot take your ring."

"Why not?" he asked.

"I am not ready to get married. I do not want to give up my job and move to New York because I enjoy doing what I'm doing."

He just sat there staring at me. He knew me well enough to know when I meant what I said and that he'd be wasting his time trying to change my mind. "Well, guess I'd better go then."

"Why not spend the day, and let's go rambling and sightseeing and then have lunch someplace?"

"No, it's best if I go on back."

I knew he could be stubborn too, so I didn't argue. He put the ring away. I looked at the box of candy regretfully. It was a beautiful box, and I loved chocolates, but I held them out to him. I didn't feel it was right to keep his candy either.

"Oh, go on and keep that, I know how you love chocolate." I didn't know whether to giggle or cry. I felt like doing both. I thought about giving him a hug, but a couple of the men boarders from downstairs, also curious, came by looking at us. He grimly stared back at them until they'd passed. "Just as well be in the railroad station," he grumbled. "Mary, I can't talk anymore right now, but I'll write you when I get home."

After he left, I did cry. I'd been too busy to think much about my old school life and my friends, but now I was mentally back in Raleigh and saw them all—Ethel, Madga, Jessie, Miss Watford, everybody, and the campus. Even if I could physically go back now, things would never be the same. Old friends would be gone. I'd be seeing the ghosts of people and times past. Besides, I had a whole new life of my own before me!

Washington was teeming with all kinds of people trying to help win this war and bring our boys home. Celebrities came from Hollywood to put on shows in Potomac Park and to sell war bonds. Captured German planes and even a submarine was put on exhibit for people to look at and understand the reality and horror of the war and put forth their best efforts to win it. The streets were full of people hurrying to and fro. Sometimes I'd stop for a red light while crossing the street, and when I'd start walking again, I would be surrounded by what seemed to be thousands of people. I knew I was only a tiny cog in this important city and in this unique period in history. I felt very humble and yet very proud that I, who some people saw only as being deaf and dumb and brainless as well, was right here in the midst of all these happenings, even a part of them. For me, it was awesome!

One day while on my way to Pennsylvania Avenue to catch the Arlington bus, I came upon a crowd of people who were just standing there waiting, filling both sides of F Street. Since it was early, I decided to wait and see what was going to happen. A small boy standing next to me looked up and smiled. I smiled back. Encouraged by this, he took hold of my hand. I looked at the lady on the other side whom I believed to be his mother. She looked at me, not smiling, but I guess she decided I looked harmless and didn't object to this new friendship. We stood and waited. I felt someone touch me from behind. I turned around and saw that it was my sister-in-law Lattice's, cousin James Henry. It was nice seeing someone from home. He asked me what we were waiting for. I said I had not the least idea. He laughed and joined the crowd but eventually got tired of waiting and moved on. I later found out that when he made a trip home, he told of seeing me with a small boy on the street and wanted to know who that little boy was. I had no idea whose child it was either. Finally, I saw action down the street. Army vehicles started passing us with decorated officers in them. We waved and cheered. Other cars passed. I don't know who, but I waved and cheered anyway. Suddenly, I felt a thrill of excitement as I was looking right at Lucille Ball. I'd seen her and her red hair on movie screens many times. Next, I recognized the Marx Brothers, then Dick Powell. He was the last one I could see go by because it was about time for the bus for Arlington to come through, and I was still two blocks away. I moved on. The stars had arrived in town for a show to help sell bonds for the war.

The day after Sonny returned to New York, I received a special delivery letter from him. It was a long letter and painful to read about how unhappy he was. I never told him I would marry him or made promises of any kind. I was eighteen years old now, legally of age, and felt my life was mine to make my own decisions. I'd been under my parents' rule, then school rules, now I was under God's rules and my own. Besides, there was something I had not told anyone. During the summer, I'd sort of met someone on the local passenger train going to visit relatives in a nearby town. There was a nice-looking boy riding to the same town. He had smiled such a sweet, friendly smile when he saw me looking at him. I looked the other way. He was a hearing person, and I had no illusions when it came to strange men and boys. I got along fine with the ones who knew me. Some of them could fingerspell, or I could read their lips. But strange boys, I'd had them notice me and start trying to get acquainted. Upon finding out I was deaf, some would turn away quickly, while others decided they'd have some fun, so they'd grin and look around to see who was enjoying the show, then wiggle their fingers and make faces. This kind I hated with a passion. I'd just give them a cool look and get on about my business, even while my hands were itching to slap their smirking faces. As for this cute guy on the train, I didn't want to find out whether or not he was like that, so I kept my face turned toward the window and ignored him. When the train stopped, I went my way and figured I'd never see him again, but that wasn't to be.

Later that summer when I was on Back Street, which was our Negro street in Wallace, I saw him again. I started to go somewhere else, but he'd seen me and came up smiling. I just stood there waiting for my sister and my friend. He started talking. I said, "I don't know you." He kept talking. Eunice and Bertha came over to see what was going on. They spoke to him and then asked me if I had seen him before. I said no and walked off. I don't know what they told him, but he left. He really was cute, quite tall, at least six feet with reddish brown hair and hazel eyes. Sometimes I thought about him and wished I could hear and not have to go through so much, but felt it was less hurtful if I shut things like that out to begin with. Now I had to deal with Sonny. I didn't want to hurt anyone's feelings, so I sat down and wrote back to let him know what a nice person he was, and how much I'd enjoyed schooldays and being his friend. I said maybe one day we could work things out and go further, but I never heard from him again. Well, that's that, I decided, and went on with my new life.

By now, it was the spring of 1943, and D.C. was beautiful. I saw the famous cherry blossoms in bloom for the first time and thought they and the Tidal Basin were the loveliest spots I'd ever seen. I passed them all, the Washington Monument, the Lincoln Memorial, and the White House, every day on my way across the river to Arlington. I loved to see the sun sparkle on the Potomac River as we crossed. At that time, once you crossed the bridge,

A card that was presented to me by the Department of the Navy
for a "perfect record for Attendance, Punctuality, Efficiency,
and Diligence" for one week.

it was open country until you reached the Navy Annex. The only
buildings were a Hot Shoppe, an old red brick building that someone said was once an electrical plant, and then there was the
Pentagon, which we would pass under. It was like a very large
tunnel or basement. Most of the passengers got off there, as the
Pentagon was a huge place, employing many people in wartime.
It was the largest building I had ever seen, and was said to have
sixteen miles of corridors.

I liked where the Navy Annex was located best. It was a long
four-story building with long wings running from the back like a
letter E, but with many more extensions than the three that appear on an E. One was a branch post office. Three had cafes,
while the others held different departments. When I first started
working, our department was on the third floor. Paperwork was
piling up and more space was needed, so a fourth floor had been
added. We came to work one evening to find that our department

had been moved upstairs, and in addition to Muster Roll, we also had miscellaneous records. Our desks had been placed in the same order as before. You'd think it was the same room, except this one was somewhat longer and there were some rafters that were still exposed.

When the weather warmed up, we soon found out that the air conditioning system wasn't completed either. Since we worked nights when the air was cooler, it really didn't matter for a while. However, when the nights became hot and windows were raised, we discovered we didn't have screens on the windows either. A bunch of window fans were brought in, and as a result, paperwork flew everywhere, unless we kept it weighted down. Night insects also came into the office to sample us and, finding that we were to their liking, brought along relatives and friends. One night a bat decided to see what was happening and flew in. We went wild shrieking and diving under our desks. At that time, we only had one man on the night shift, Mr. Gaskins. He tried to be manly and shoo the bat back outside, but all that creature would do was fly the length of the room, making a low swoop over the center, and fly back to the other end. I made myself comfortable under my desk and prepared to stay there as long as necessary. Finally, Raymond stooped and told me to come on out, saying that the bat had settled on a rafter and looked as if he planned to spend the night. We went back to work, but kept an eye out for our latest visitor.

Soon after this, screens covered the windows, and the ceiling was also finished. Since this room was longer than the one on the third floor, more tables and desks were added to the other end and more workers were hired to open and sort mail. Among these was a motherly looking lady named Mrs. L. B. Moore. I liked her at once and she seemed to be quite interested in me. One night at snack time, she invited me to sit with her. We found a spot at one of the mail tables. She believed in eating hearty and had brought food from home, which she offered to share with me, and I graciously accepted a deviled egg. It was very good. We started getting acquainted. She was a native of Wilmington, North Carolina. Her husband had died, so she'd moved to D.C. and was living with a nephew. I told her about my family and about Wallace. She became quiet and then took paper and pencil and wrote a little note to see if I'd mind her asking me a personal question.

"Like what?" I asked her.

She studied awhile, then wrote another note asking how I had lost my hearing. I didn't mind telling her that. I told her how I had lost it gradually when I was in the fourth grade. She said she thought that it was remarkable that I was out there working with the rest of the people. I laughed and told her there was nothing remarkable about it. The deaf were people too and had to eat and live like any anyone else. I explained that deaf people wanted the chance to work for a living. We became good friends. She called me Mary, and I called her L. B.

Also hired at this time was a girl about my age named Rhoda. This was her senior year in high school, and she was working nights and going to school during the day. She lived with her family on P Street, not far from N Street. She was putting money aside to help pay her way to college. Rhoda was so much like the kids at home. We had the same kind of upbringing, going to church, and so on. We were soon doing things together—going to lunch, for snacks. L. B. took Rhoda in too and tried to mother both of us. Rhoda and I were the youngest on the force, and some called us the office babies. I soon found out that, like everywhere else, the people here were class-conscious. The upper crust were the bosses and supervisors, then came the ex-school teachers and professionals. Next, there was a group of young single adults who liked to go to the clubs on U Street when they got off at night and party. The housewives and mothers with children made up the last group. I didn't fit into either one, so I just took them all as I found them. If they acted friendly toward me I treated them likewise; if not, I left them alone. It didn't bother me one way or the other.

My brother-in-law's construction job in Richmond had ended, and Eunice wanted to try life in D.C. They stayed at Cousin Mary's until they found a small apartment in Arlington, which was just down Columbia Pike from where I worked. It just made my day having my sister in Washington with me. She joined me in exploring the city. She loved the clothing stores. I still loved the small shops and the outdoor market. Cousin Mary wanted Eunice to take the civil service test and get a government job. She said she didn't want a government job and soon found one to her liking, making salads in a Chinese restaurant. She loved working with food. She was off on Sundays, but her employer would send her a full-course Chinese dinner. This was new to me. I liked the fried noodles, rice, and chicken, but the other stuff looked strange. One Sunday Eunice and I, along with Leroy and a few more folks, decided to walk down to Pennsylvania Avenue and visit the museums and the Smithsonian Institution. It was really awesome. We saw evening gowns that the presidents' wives had worn, a gold piano, things dating back in history showing us how people had lived, beautiful paintings, and jewelry, the shell of a huge turtle and skeletons of other animals including a dinosaur. From there we crossed over to see the first airplane, antique cars, and other things. We couldn't take it all in that day. I told myself that one day I was going back early and take the whole day to look at everything.

Meanwhile, the war wore on. Each day the papers ran a column with the number of American boys who'd been killed that day, or who had been wounded or captured, and who was missing in action. The newspapers only gave numbers because the families of the dead soldiers had yet to be notified. Telegrams arrived at different homes bringing heartbreaking messages. Not all citizens had Social Security cards, but they sure had ration books. Our boys in service had to have the best of everything. They needed leather for sturdy shoes and boots to protect their feet. Thus, ordinary citizens were allowed to purchase only three pairs of real leather shoes a year. We could buy as many pairs of canvas shoes and sandals as we wanted. We called them play shoes for some reason. Silk was needed for parachutes, so no more sheer silk stockings. We had to wear heavy rayon or fishnet, and in summer, some women bought a deep tan lotion, covered their legs with it, and had "birthday" stockings. Each person was allowed just so much meat, butter, gas, and other things. If anyone complained, I was not aware of it. Everyone seemed willing and glad to give up anything for our boys. It seemed that all of America was a hundred percent behind them and ready to do whatever was necessary to bring them home again.

I had two brothers out there. Willie was still in Texas at an air base, but Bennie, the older one, who was married and had three little girls, was in the middle of some of the worst fighting in Europe. Churches were serving meals to servicemen who happened to be in town or on leave. Women were asked to go to USOs to talk or dance with the servicemen, or write letters, and befriend the boys. My brothers, cousins, and friends asked me to write some of the guys in their company who didn't get mail from home, and gave me their addresses. As a result, I was always getting letters from people I'd never heard of, and I answered them all.

One day I picked up a letter from Salt Lake City. When I opened it, it said "Gotcha!" I was surprised at this. Upon reading further, I realized that it was from the cute boy on the train, no less! He was in the same company as one of my favorite cousins. He saw a picture of me and got my address. He said he knew I wouldn't refuse to write him now that he was in service, even though I wouldn't talk to him before. I wrote back that I had a reason for not talking to strange boys, because I was deaf and didn't want any problems. He answered right back, with a very nice letter and never referred to my being deaf, which was his way of letting me know it didn't matter. From then on, he wrote to me at least twice a week and sometimes more.

My brothers also wrote me often. Willie always wanted to get out of Texas before he was cooked, it was so hot. Bennie was in England and wrote about how beautiful the English countryside was. It was early summer and the city was becoming hot. One Sunday when Cousin Kinch was off from work, Cousin Mary cooked up a big lunch and we all rode up to Rock Creek Park for a picnic and then visited the zoo. This was the first large park I'd ever been to, and it felt good being among trees, grass, and flowers. When we packed up to go home, Leroy, Elnora, and I, along with a few of their friends, decided to walk home. The park was quite a distance from N Street. The others told us we would get mighty tired. We said we could always catch a streetcar. We set out walking. We laughed and played and had fun. It was nearly dusk when we reached N Street, and we kept right on going all the way to the Tidal Basin, down past Pennsylvania Avenue. We sat on the grass under the cherry trees. It was cool and pleasant. A lot of other people had the same idea and started coming in with blankets and children. After a while we decided to walk back up to our own neighborhood, and to bed!

# 5

# A Place of My Own

*. . . let us be true*
*To one another! for the world, which seems*
*To lie before us like a land of dreams,*
*So various, so beautiful, so new . . .*

Matthew Arnold,
"Dover Beach"

BY NOW, Eunice and R. C. were living in their new apartment. I had gone with them to see it before they moved in, and I fell in love with the place. It was quiet and old-timey. The house had been built way back, probably in the 1800s. It was large and had back stairs as well as front stairs and funny little nooks and crannies. I wanted to move in with them, but their place only had one bedroom. Their landlord was Reverend Chapman. He and his wife had no children, so they'd had the second floor remodeled into two apartments. Another couple had the other one. We started looking for a place for me. A lady down the street rented all of her second floor to working girls, but she was filled up. However, she referred me to her sister-in-law, Mrs. Jeanette

Mosely, just across the street from Eunice. When Eunice and I went to see it, she was pleasant and said she'd let me know the next day. When we went back, she was smiling and said yes, I could rent the room. In fact, she'd already decided when she was talking with me the day before. She said she was just going through the motions. No one lived there besides herself, her husband, and her two adult children, a son and daughter.

She took me upstairs to see the room. It was large and airy with a double bed, a dresser, a desk, a chair, and a comfortable-looking hassock. One window looked out on a large oak tree in one corner of the yard. The other showed a good view of the D.C. skyline, including the dome on the Capitol. Her daughter's room was right beside it, and her son's room was across the stair landing. Both were on the front. I absolutely loved it. Downstairs was a kitchen, a living room, a dining room, and her and Mr. Mosely's rooms, along with a sun porch, a side porch, and back and front porches. The rent for that big, clean, comfortable room, which is hard to believe now, was only four dollars a week. One dollar extra would cover freshly laundered bedclothes every Friday and kitchen privileges. I could also use her washing machine in the basement and iron my personal things. The living room and dining room could be used for any guests I had. Everything was spotless but gave you an "at home" feeling. She said that men were not allowed in the bedroom.

"Don't worry," I said, "we couldn't have done that at home either, even if we'd wanted to. Besides," I added, "I don't even have a boyfriend—at least nowhere near here."

She said she could tell Eunice and I were well-raised girls as soon as she talked with us. Mama would just love to hear that. And so I moved to Scott Street in South Arlington, Virginia. It was sad leaving Cousin Mary and her family, but she understood that I wanted to be near Eunice and to be able to walk to and from work. The Annex was only a couple of blocks away down Columbia Pike, and also, I'd come to visit on Sundays or just about any other day. We'd still be close and I'd still love them. The other two girls who'd stayed there had also moved out. One married a serviceman, and the other had cousins on U Street and moved near them. Now Cousin Mary's oldest daughter, who'd been in New Jersey, had moved back to D.C. and worked in the Treasury Building. It worked out fine for all of us, because now Georgia would have her bedroom back and I would be close to work and in an area with lots of grass and trees. A city girl, I was not.

Some Sunday evenings at Cousin Mary's, when there was nothing to do and the family would be about their own business, Eunice and I would sit out front on the doorstep watching people hurry by. The steps started right at the walk, so close we could have reached out and touched someone, yet, we could have been invisible for all of the attention anyone paid us. Women tripped by with high heels tapping and fancy hairdos with flowers riding on their heads. Sometimes my sister and I would look at each other and see that the other was homesick too. We'd say if we were home we would probably be out to Cousin Bert's or in Wallace someplace. "Or walking the road to the creek," I added. "These people are sure stuck-up. Can't even say howdy or smile when they pass by." We didn't know city ways then. Sometimes we'd walk over to Seventh Street and window-shop, or stop someplace for a root beer and a hot dog. Now, I was out here in Arlington where people had gardens and fruit trees, went to church on Sundays, and would speak.

Although I missed the Fennell family, especially Cousin Mary and Leroy, I was tickled to pieces with my new abode. I changed the furniture around more to my liking, putting the bed where I could look out at the branches of the large oak tree. I could also see the windows of Eunice's apartment across the street. Mrs.

Mosely helped me get acquainted with my surroundings. The street running in front of her house from the pike was Scott Street. Rolfe Street ran down past the side for a block, then curved out onto Columbia Pike, the big main street. She pointed out her mother's house right at the bend in the street—a tall narrow white house with a porch across the front. The one next-door to it, a single-story house, was her sister's. Across the way, toward Washington on a hilltop, was a small white wood church. This was their family church (Baptist), where Mrs. Mosley was choir director. The stores were further down the pike, just a couple of blocks. I could either catch a bus at the end of Scott Street or walk, and it wasn't far.

The large white house across the street and about one door downbelonged to her husband's brother and his wife, Miss Emmy. She'd added, "She dips snuff," and made a face. I laughed at that and thought of my mom's dislike of snuff. Directly across the street in front of her house was a large, well-kept vegetable garden. That was hers. The rest of the street was pretty empty until you reached the end, where there was another tall narrow house. An old lady lived there alone. It was a perfect picture of a Halloween haunted house. The house behind us was tan stucco with a red tile roof. It looked Spanish, out of place among all these other houses that dated back to Civil War days. I loved to look down on it from the window in my room. There was a rosebush in the nearest corner with the largest and prettiest pink roses I had ever seen.

Next, I ventured down to Arlington Village to buy groceries, not knowing the distance. I caught the bus at the corner of Scott and Columbia. The village was like looking at a picture. There were two small grocery stores, a drugstore, a post office, a gift shop, and a few more buildings. If you needed to see a dentist or buy clothes or see a movie, you had to ride across the river to

D.C. It was a very nice homey-looking little village. The grocery store was like the ones in Wallace where they had glass meat cases. You were able to look the meat over and pick out what you wanted. A clerk weighed it and wrapped it up and marked the price on it. The only meat you could get without a ration coupon was wieners, chicken, and lunchmeat. I thought about it and decided that I wasn't about to eat a whole chicken. They didn't come cut up and packaged at that time. I'd get my main meal at the Annex and just eat light things at home. I stocked up with bread, peanut butter, jelly, cheese crackers, fruit, and such. I was getting a quart of milk delivered to the house three times a week. Those were milkman days. Since my bag wasn't heavy, I decided to walk back to Scott Street. The left side I was on was lined with nice single-family homes like in Wallace with large lawns and lots of trees and flowers, and like Wallace, only the whites lived there. On the right side were red brick apartments, duplexes, and small single-family homes that extended for a block or so, and then there were lots of white wood barracks-type buildings. This extended until you reached Scott Street. I found out that the brick homes were for the naval and marine officers and their families. The white buildings were for naval and marine enlisted men and their families. For the rest of the way, from Scott Street on to an intersection, homes that Blacks lived in were on both sides of the pike and were just as nice as the rest.

Mrs. Mosely cleared out a shelf in her refrigerator and three shelves in the cabinet for me to keep my food. She showed me how to light her gas stove, both top and oven. I already had a key to my room. Her daughter's name was Doretha. She had taught fourth grade at an elementary school across the pike but had left teaching for an office job in the Department of Agriculture. The son's name was Andrew. He and Mr. Mosely did construction work, and Mrs. Mosely gave piano lessons in her home and studied music at a conservatory in D.C. They were a nice, busy family. When I informed my friends at work that I had moved to Arlington, they were alarmed at first, wanting to know if I had checked out the people I'd moved in with, but they calmed down when I told them my sister was close by. It's nice to have friends who care.

I walked to work and found there was a back gate, which opened to the pike. I could go right on in and enter through the post office wing. That put me right near the elevator we used, and I didn't have to pass through the lobby. It only took me about five or ten minutes to arrive at my desk after leaving home. I was a fast walker, like my papa. Two other workers also lived in Arlington, right there on the pike, and the three of us walked home together the first couple of nights. That was how I became friends with Doggett and Choisey. For a while, I had been riding home with Lucy, one of the young singles. She had a steady boyfriend who worked in a garage. He'd drive all the way to the Annex in a yellow company truck to pick Lucy up. Since they went past N Street, she'd asked me if I would like to ride with her. I gladly accepted. It was much quicker than the bus and streetcars. Lucy and her boyfriend were fun and we had lots of laughs. I told her about my new arrangements and thanked her for her kindness. A man on day shift, Mr. Mainor, was switched to night shift. He lived one street from Choisey and Doggett, so he let us all ride with him.

No one waited up for me at Mrs. Mosely's house. Everyone would be asleep. A key was left for me so that I could get in. My mail would be on a table in the hall by the front door. After I put on my nightclothes, I would go down to the kitchen, fix a snack, then carry it to my room, sit at the desk, and open my mail. Usually there would be lots of mail to open. Some mail was from home, but mostly it was from the pen pals I had in the service.

They didn't have to put stamps on their mail. They could write as often as they liked and not have to worry about buying stamps. I didn't mind buying stamps. They didn't cost so much then, just three or four cents, I think. Anyway, I really enjoyed writing them. Some were still in the States, while others were in foreign countries. They would tell me about the people, their customs, and the food they ate. It was very interesting. Some were in the actual fighting and couldn't say where they were. Sometimes they'd be in foxholes, wet and scared. One, whose letters I enjoyed the most, was Mickey. No matter where he was, he could always find something funny to write about and make you laugh. In one letter he wasn't laughing because the girl he had left back home had died from food poisoning. He was from Louisiana. Another was from Florida and sent me a whole crate of oranges for Christmas.

Some of the girls asked me if I would like to go to the USO with them sometime. I said no, I was too busy writing the boys who were a long way off. As for my job at the Annex, I had nothing to complain about. I loved it and liked the people I worked with. We had three more males in the office now. They'd hired two boys and a middle-aged man who was from New York. His name was Joe. I think the two boys were just out of high school and waiting to be drafted. One was named Corbin, and the other was Greg. They helped on the mail end. I was also getting a bit of a social life. One of our single girls—we called them the midnight howlers—invited Rhoda and me to her apartment for lunch and a movie before time to go to work. She lived uptown, so Rhoda met me, and we found her apartment on W Street. It was a nice apartment. She and her mom lived together. After a nice lunch, we met another girl, Murphy, and all of us went to the Howard Theater. This was big-time for Blacks. They featured a stage show with a big-name band or singers before showing the film. That day it was Louis Prima's band. Shortly after that, Rhoda had a birthday party. I was invited to that and told to bring Leroy with me. The party was like the ones we had at home. All of the family attended, young and old. She had a large birthday cake and ice cream. Her mom was a sweet-faced little lady. I also went to church with Rhoda one Sunday and met her pastor, and went with her to communion one Sunday night. The service was beautiful, and I enjoyed it so much. It was done by candlelight.

This may sound like my life was perfect and I was always happy, but that was definitely not the case. There were still times when I was made to feel my deafness; most of the time it wasn't intentional, but the hurt was there just the same. For instance, once during break time a bunch of us were talking about the USO and the requests for women and girls to attend a dance they were having for the service boys. They needed someone to dance with and talk to. One member of the group I had seen watching me several times, as though she was curious about me or something, looked at me then and said, "You people don't dance, do you?"

"Yes, we can." I said.

"But how?" she asked.

"With our feet," I said.

The others laughed, and she gave me a sour look. I waited for more questions, but none came. We went back to work. There were other incidents, but I learned to live with them. That was a part of my life, which would always be with me from time to time, and I decided I wouldn't let it throw me. I wondered if she said "you people" because she thought we were a separate part of the human race. After that, she always spoke and acted pleasant, but never asked me any more questions. Two other girls she was close friends with, Johnson and Laura, were very friendly, and I felt comfortable with them. Johnson was quite pretty and Laura's looks were striking as well. She was very dark with a nice shape. She had long black hair and her eyes always looked sleepy. She wore beautiful clothes.

Speaking of clothes, one day Rhoda and I decided to go shopping early. We started with the downtown stores. When we got to Woodward and Lothrop, I was in for another new experience. From the store entrance, we entered a large room with very soft, thick carpet. There were nice living room couches and chairs, shaded lamps, flowers, and mirrors, but no dresses. I saw no people either. I looked around. Was this a store? I turned to look at Rhoda and saw that a neatly dressed lady had appeared from someplace to see what we wanted. Rhoda asked what type of dress I wanted to look at. I hadn't even thought about a type. I was used to going through the racks until I found one I liked. Now I just said something for Easter. After we gave her our sizes, the lady started walking off, and I followed right behind her. I meant to see all of the dresses. Rhoda grabbed my jacket and pulled me back. We sat on one of the couches until she finally came back with some dresses hanging over her arm. None of them were to my or Rhoda's liking. I don't think that lady wanted to sell two young Black girls any of those high-priced clothes.

I said, "Let's go to Hecht and Lansburg." Cousin Mary had taken me to Hecht last Easter, and I'd found a beautiful pale blue dress, a navy spring coat, shoes, and bag, plus a tiny hat that seemed no more than a bunch of flowers with a wispy veil. It cost more than anything I'd ever had before, but I was making my own money now and could splurge a little. Now, it was too late to go any farther. We stopped at a diner for lunch then went on to work.

We got our paychecks every two weeks. I worked out a budget. I'd give Mrs. Mosely two weeks' rent, which was ten dollars. I allowed so much for food, carfare, lunches, and some for Mama and Papa, pocket change for spending, and the rest I put into savings by buying twenty-five-dollar war bonds. Sam was still in school. I bought him a plaid sports jacket, and dresses for Mama and Eunice.

As much as I enjoyed Cousin Mary and her family, it always felt good to be back in my room at night, large and homey. Come to think of it, this was the first time in my life I'd had an entire room to myself. At home, I had shared a room with Eunice. At school, rooms were shared with all those other girls. At Cousin Mary's, there'd been Sidney, another girl from down home. The war wore on; grim news was coming over the radio and in the newspaper. I brought a *Herald* newspaper every day, so I could keep up with it on my own, and I continued to pray for all those I knew to make it back home safely. Maleon and I were writing each other steadily now. We shared so much. He had been majoring in music in college when he was drafted, and he loved it as much as I did when I could still hear. We both loved to read and liked the same movies. Most of all, we had the same hope of one day having a large comfortable home in the country, someplace with a big stone fireplace. We weren't making any plans yet. The war made everything uncertain, but as he said, we can dream can't we?

One of my cousins wrote me a frantic letter. His girl back home had run away, and he couldn't locate her. He thought she might be with me or at least might have told me where she was going, since we were good friends. I had no idea. She had sent a message saying she'd be in D.C. one night and told me what time to meet the bus, but she never showed up, and I'd heard no more from her. He finally located his girlfriend in Delaware. It might have been better if she'd stayed missing because she now had someone else.

That cousin was stationed at Fort Hood, Texas. A company from there was scheduled to put on a show someplace in Potomac

Maleon when he was a student at North Carolina Agricultural and Technical State University.

Park to sell war bonds shortly after that time. Leroy, Elnora, and I went to see the show. It was very good, but my cousin wasn't there. Sometimes one of our boys overseas would be shot down or killed in some other way. If it was big news, we'd watch to see if he'd be buried in Arlington, and if so, on what day. Mr. Gaskins said those who wished to do so could go to the window and watch the funeral. The grave would have been dug early in the day, and then you'd see the procession coming slowly through the cemetery. From the chapel, further toward the back, the casket would be on a wagon or caisson, pulled by horses. There'd only be the officers and family members in attendance. The women in the family usually wore black with long black veils over their heads and faces. The saddest part was when they fired the guns over the grave and played Taps. The whole office would be lined up at the windows, all looking sad and solemn as though it was someone we knew. Whether Black or White, the dead boy was young and had given up his life for our country. Their families were heartbroken. Sometimes I'd stand there for a long time, thinking of how I would feel if that was one of the people I loved.

When I looked around, the rest of the staff would be back at work. Then I'd scuttle back to my desk, but Mr. Gaskins never said anything. I didn't want to lose my status.

Some of the big brass naval officers had started a project called the "gold star" employees. Admiral Breedlove was over our department. Each Friday he and another officer, Ensign Keating, would come to our office to meet with all who had come to work on time each night, worked diligently, and been cooperative. These employees were called up and given a card with a gold star on it. At the end of the month, whoever had four gold stars was given a certificate. This helped to determine who got raises and promotions. I hadn't missed a week yet getting a star. My stars were piling up.

I still went over to Cousin Mary's a couple of days a week. Sometimes Eunice went with me. She and I had met and made friends with the girls who lived down the street at Miss Emmy's house. They were all from West Virginia. One girl had a boyfriend who had been drafted and sent to nearby Fort Myer, Virginia. She followed him, found a room as close to him as possible, and then found a job. Her sister, Sarah, followed her, then two or three of her cousins also followed. They all had jobs working together at the Pentagon in housekeeping. They said where they came from was coal-mining country, and it was very hard to make a living. They had all of the second floor of Miss Emmy's house except her own bedroom. It was a large rambling house with a back staircase. The girls worked at night, so Eunice and I spent many happy hours laughing and talking with them. There was another one from North Carolina named Maggie. Being that she was from the South and was also Baptist, she had started attending St. John's Baptist Church, just a few doors down on the corner. Eunice and I went with her to church one Sunday. We had to stand up to be introduced as guests. I was so busy looking at someone in front of me I forgot to sit back down, until Eunice pulled on my dress tails. Anyway, we enjoyed church and were invited to come back. No matter where we went, we still remembered our religion and our church back home.

Memorial Day rolled around, and one of the office girls who had found a room in Arlington, across the pike, asked me what I'd be doing that day. I told her I had nothing planned.

"Let's go see the president put a wreath on the Tomb of the Unknown Soldier," she suggested.

"Great! I'd love that!" I was always ready for a new adventure. This was Sylvia. I hadn't had much contact with her because by her being a "super," she was in the bosses' group. She turned out to be a really kind, down-to-earth sort of person. I found my way to her room on Thirteenth Street. Her room was in a neat, new brick home. All the houses in that section were built more or less alike, with small patches of grass. Some were fenced in. Her room was also up-to-date in pink and white with polished hardwood floors. I still liked my homey room and all those old-fashioned houses best.

We set out walking to the cemetery. It was only a couple of blocks away. There was quite a large crowd gathered at the amphitheater. I was surprised to see that it had no roof, but had windows all around, stone benches, and a stage. Someone was on the stage speaking when we entered, but was soon finished. Everyone went out behind the building to where the tomb was located. I was fascinated watching the soldier who was on duty as he guarded the tomb, pacing back and forth. He'd get to one end, stop, turn smartly, clicking his heels, then march slowly back to the other end. We saw them change guards while waiting for the wreath to arrive. It wasn't President Roosevelt who placed the wreath, but someone who represented him. It was a beautiful ceremony and quite moving. I thought of that soldier lying there dead and no one to claim him, to make sure he wasn't left there to just waste away. He had to have had a mom and dad at sometime or other. I wondered, didn't someone wonder where he was when the war was over and grieve for him. I thought of Bennie and Willie and Leon and the others I knew. They'd be missed terribly. I couldn't even think about it. The crowd was breaking up and leaving now. Sylvia and I walked past the Curtis Lee House.

"We'll come back one day and visit this place too," she told me. Since she was from New York City, she'd never seen any of this either. I saw one man watching everything perched in a tree.

When I returned home and told Mrs. Mosely where I'd been, she looked disapproving and said, "You went up there? I've never been out there and I'm not going."

I was surprised, and asked her why not. She said she didn't know who was in that tomb, but everybody believed he was White. "Well," I said, "I don't think it really matters what color he was; he could have been Black, but the thing is that he died for our country."

She asked if I had seen any Black people there besides myself and Sylvia. I thought back and couldn't remember seeing any, except the man or boy in the tree, who had looked sort of brown. "That's because they don't go to such things here," she told me. I've never understood that. Mrs. Mosely was a kind, easygoing, Christian lady in every way except when it came to questions of race and morals.

Cousin Mary hadn't given up on having something done about my hearing. She paid another visit to a rehabilitation office on New York Avenue and told them I should have a hearing aid, even though the doctors had said that wouldn't help my deafness. But, being Cousin Mary, she'd convinced someone that's what I needed. So one day a call came to Mrs. Mosely's house for me to expect someone to bring a hearing aid out there to fit on me. It turned out to be a young White male. He was pleasant and polite. Nevertheless, after letting him in and coming upstairs to get me, Mrs. Mosley stood grimly in the doorway and watched his every move. He explained to me how to put the hearing aid on. He didn't dare help me, what with Mrs. Mosely's eyes on him.

Compared to today's hearing aids, this thing was monstrous. It consisted of a battery pack about the size of a thick deck of cards and wires that ran from the battery pack to a slightly smaller pack that was the motor, I guess. Then, there was another wire that ran from this smaller pack with a small rubber piece attached to the end. This was then inserted into one ear. Once he had the hearing aid in place, he shook my hand, wished me luck, and took his departure quite hastily. I really didn't want the thing. All it did was tingle and make noises that were nerve-wracking. Mrs. Mosely and I examined it and tried to see if it helped my hearing any. It didn't. She said that maybe if I wore it awhile that it would get better. She then asked if I had minded that she had stayed in the room while the hearing aid man was there.

I said, "Not really, it's your house."

"You weren't scared to be alone with him?"

"No, ma'am, I am used to talking with White people at home and at school. None of them ever tried to harm me."

"Well, I don't trust them," she said.

I put the hearing aid away but tried wearing it while in my room to see if it would get better, and it didn't. One day I decided to wear it when I went to the village for groceries. Since it was raining, I took the bus. Two small White boys, who I paid no mind, came back and sat beside me. Then I realized they were trying to see inside my ears. The contraption was making a noise that others could hear. I thought for a few minutes, then reached up and removed the end piece and showed it to them.

"That's a hearing aid," I said, grinning at their surprised look. "I'm deaf." I remembered my own curiosity as a child. I never wore it anywhere else again.

Now, our part of the country was having blackouts. From some unknown place, a loud siren would go off, and all lights everywhere went out. There were air raid wardens, who walked the streets in dark clothes. If they saw one speck of light in a house, they would bang on the door and order you to put that light out. You could be fined if you didn't obey their orders. We never knew when or what time a drill would come. The Germans were sending bombs into England. We were being trained to be prepared and not to give them a target to shoot at. Looking out the window across the river, all of D.C. was pitch black, as was all our area.

I was still enjoying the work I was doing. It was summer again, and the days were long and hot. Sometime between checking in and lunch or dinnertime, I'd find myself getting drowsy. A couple of times, Raymond rolled her chair close enough to reach over and touch me. I'd jerk awake and find I'd been making scratches on my reports instead of checks. I went to the restroom, splashed cold water on my face, and then stopped by the water fountain to drink ice water. There were two ladies' rooms on our end of the corridor. The sign on the door only said "Ladies' Restroom," without having White or Colored added. However, one was a little larger with nicer chairs and mirrors than those in the other room. The White women would use it to take breaks, smoke cigarettes, and give the Black women hard stares when we went in there. Some would even say to us, "There's another restroom further down." Most of the girls pretended that they didn't hear them and just continued to use the ladies' room. Then signs started appearing in different places saying that all facilities, restrooms, cafes, and so on were to be used by *all* government employees regardless of race, color, or creed. After that, no one bothered us, but we still got bad looks from a few; that didn't hurt at all.

I think Mrs. Roosevelt was behind a lot of the changes that were taking place. At first Black servicemen could not go in USOs where the Whites went, but I read in the news that a nice new USO was being built in D.C. and that it would be for both races. It was reported that on opening night, Mrs. Roosevelt was there dancing with a Black serviceman while the band played "Let Me Call You Sweetheart." It didn't seem to bother Mrs. Roosevelt in the least. She kept on with whatever she was doing, visiting prisoners and other places. I always thought of her as being a great lady.

I think I mentioned there being a small grocery store beside our building. It was outside the fence and across the street, but we could go out there for things that were not sold in the Annex. Popsicles were one of those things. Since it was hot, several of us would run across and buy for all the rest. One day, I went with a couple of the other girls, and we came in from a different way. Standing guard at the corridor was one of the handsomest men I'd ever seen. I didn't know his race. He could have been Black, White, Indian, or Spanish. The other girls must have seen him before and didn't seem at all impressed. They just flashed their tags and kept on going. I held up my lopsided tag, but he didn't look at it; he was looking at me. I thought, oh mercy what did I do, and almost ran into a wall, when I had to turn a corner. I looked back and found that he was still watching me. It was a while before I saw him again, as we didn't use that particular entrance much. However, one day another girl, Frances, and I went to get the treats and came back in that way, and there he was again. I had taken the cover off my Popsicle and was preparing to eat it. He was looking at me again and actually asked me for a piece of my Popsicle. I pushed the whole thing toward him and blurted, "You can have it."

He laughed and said, "No just a piece." Breaking off half, he handed the rest back to me.

From that point on, I stopped taking that route. I did ask Jones about him and what race he was. She didn't know but said he was probably Spanish since there were many more in the building. One day, Eunice and I had been to Cousin Mary's to visit and had to go to someplace on New York Avenue. While standing on the corner of Eleventh and N Street waiting for traffic to pass so we could get to the island to wait for the streetcar, a taxi stopped directly in front of us. The driver was a friendly-looking Black boy who asked if we wanted a ride. I looked at Eunice, she looked at me, and we nodded and got in the backseat. The driver chatted all the way, telling his name and that he was from Cuba. This was his first job, he said, and he was trying to make it successful. Eunice told him we came from North Carolina. When we arrived at our destination and asked how much the fare was, he said nothing. We thanked him and got out.

"Who is your friend, Eunice?" I asked her.

She stopped, looked at me, and said that's what she was fixing to ask me. She thought it was someone I knew. There's a saying that God looks out for babes and fools. To my knowledge, that was the only time we ever saw this person. While living on N Street, I'd discovered that I didn't really have to travel down Eleventh Street to reach Pennsylvania Avenue. I found that I could just turn the corner at Tenth after leaving Cousin Mary's house and walk straight down. Streetcars and buses didn't travel Tenth Street, so it was easier walking because it was pleasant and shady.

One day, I noticed a girl that I'd seen at the Annex leaving a house on Tenth Street as I passed by. She started walking beside me and talking. I told her I was deaf. She was surprised, but she knew how to make herself understood. Her name was Phyllis, and she worked as a keypunch operator on a different floor. She was from New York and had grown up with Frank Sinatra. They'd been friends in school, and he had told her that if he got to be a star, he would remember her. He did become a star, and everywhere he went, the teenagers, or bobby-soxers as they were called, fainted and fought over him. He kept his word, because each time a new album was released by him, he'd autograph one and send it to Phyllis. When I'd stop by her room to walk down to the Avenue, she would always be playing one of his records on a portable phonograph. He also sent her a large autographed photo of himself. That's one reason I liked him through the years. He didn't seem to choose his friends because of race, good looks, or riches. Phyllis was an average, dark-complexioned person, but nonetheless, he remembered her. She and I stayed friends until she requested to be transferred back to New York. She missed New York.

Most of the New Yorkers said D.C. was dull and too far south, and that there was nothing happening that was fun. I thought Washington was the most exciting city in the United States, and I didn't want to go any further north, as it suited me just fine. The other southerners felt the same way. During the time I'd been walking down to Pennsylvania Avenue, I'd discovered a section of M Street called Embassy Row. It's where the embassies for foreign countries were located. I'd also noticed a plain red brick building that I had to pass on Tenth Street. There was a plaque by the door, but I never stopped to read what it said. One day I decided to see who lived there or what made this building special. You can imagine my surprise to find this was Ford's Theater, the very spot where Abraham Lincoln had been shot. Looking across the street, I saw the house where they said he'd been carried to try to save his life. I thought, "Well bless old Bess, is this for real?" Here I was standing on history. I was so thrilled I had to tell somebody, but everybody I carried my great discovery to just smiled at me and said, "Really?" or something like that. I seemed to be the only one who was impressed.

I still went over to town often to visit with Cousin Mary and to walk with Leroy, Elnora, and some of their friends on Sundays. Two more kids had joined us: Billy (I think Elnora liked him), and Carmelita, a Spanish girl. She was supposedly Leroy's girlfriend, but he wouldn't walk beside her. She had very long hair that grew to below her waist, and she was quite pretty. She attracted attention along the streets. Leroy didn't like to be noticed himself, so he walked with me and Elnora, while the other boys walked behind. They reminded me of the kids back home.

# 6

# *Happy with My Life*

*Then be not coy, but use your time,*
*And, while ye may, go marry;*
*For, having lost but once your prime,*
*You may forever tarry.*

Robert Herrick,
"To the Virgins, to Make Much of Time"

SUMMER was wearing on, and we had fun. Mama wrote to tell me that Sam was catching the bus to see me and what time someone needed to meet him. I was overjoyed to hear this, because I missed my baby brother and our time together, both good and bad, meaning play time and fight time. Eunice and R. C. picked Sam up while I was still at work, so I didn't see him until the next morning. Since he was my brother, it was okay with Mrs. Mosely if he was in my room. She'd met Leroy also and made him welcome. I couldn't wait to show Arlington Village to Sam. Leroy came over, and we rambled until I had to go to work; then Sam went back across the street to Eunice's apartment, where he was staying.

The next day I had an appointment with an eye doctor in town, and Sam went with me. It was such fun having him there to ride the different modes of transportation with me. We took the bus to Pennsylvania Avenue, and from there we transferred to a streetcar to M Street, and then to another streetcar going north-northeast. Sam was beginning to look a little worried at all the changes and asked me if I was sure I knew where I was going. "Yes, I know where I'm going." I was proud for him to see that I could get around on my own in a large city. We finally reached Dr. Watson's office. After the doctor had checked my eyes, he made another appointment for me and we left. I was being fitted with glasses. This time I took Sam by a different route, to Cousin Mary's house, where he met the rest of her children. By then it was time for me to get back across the river and go to work. Sam spent a week with us.

Eunice and R. C. were driving him back home because R. C.'s job had ended for the time being. I was able to get a day or two off and went along as well. The car was a convertible. We called the backseat a rumble seat. That's where Sam and I sat. At that time, the highway leading down south was Highway 301. Oh, the fun we had riding with the top down and the wind blowing in our faces! We laughed and played, ate snacks, and waved at people as we passed by. This was surely strange behavior for adults, but we were happy that afternoon. As it got later and we got farther down Highway 301, we started seeing the edge of a dark cloud low in the west. It didn't dampen our spirits then. However, as we neared Richmond, the cloud rose higher, and the sun disappeared.

I said, "Uh-oh, look what's coming."

It wasn't too long before the cloud was overhead, very dark and very heavy. Rain started falling, so R. C. pulled off the highway and put the top up. It rained harder and harder and was almost nighttime. Sam and I had to get in the front seat, as the roof didn't cover the rumble seat. All four of us sat squeezed in together. It was then we discovered that the top had holes, and drops of rain started to come through. R. C. picked up speed with the car, trying to make it to Richmond, where they used to live. Eunice said we could visit Mrs. Mathis until the rain slacked up. However, upon reaching the place where they used to live, it seemed that one or both of the elderly couple was very sick. We decided to keep going. By now, the rain was really pouring down, while it thundered and lightninged regularly. Water had now started to trickle down our necks. Remembering that I had my umbrella with me, I let it up over my and Eunice's heads. Sam got behind us, so it covered him too. We had a good laugh at how we looked riding inside a car with an umbrella over our heads. We plodded on through the storm, bent on getting home. By the time we rolled into the yard, the rain had settled to a steady drizzle, with only an occasional flash of lightning. Everyone had gone to bed but got up to welcome us home and laughed at the way we'd had to ride under two coverings. This was on Friday night, and I had to be back to work Monday, which meant that I had to leave on Sunday evening. It was good to be home, even for this short period of time.

Mama was just as anxious to hear of my daily happenings as Cousin Mary, and she let me know that she was very proud of me. She also said that the money I was sending home was helping out a lot. That made me feel good. The kids were growing. Maxine was about three years old, and her little sister Marion, or Nod, as we called her, was a pretty baby with short curly black hair. On this visit, I didn't have time to get to Pender County and see Bennie and his family. My sister wasn't going back right then, so I had to make the return trip alone. It was okay for this time. I watched again for my old school, and when we passed it, I looked for as long as I could and again felt nostalgia for past days and old friends.

As soon as I got back to Arlington, I had to go out on the pike to my doctor's office for a sick slip to carry in. We had fourteen days of annual leave a year and as many sick days as were reasonable, without having a cut in pay. Since I was having eye problems, the doctor told me to get a note from Dr. Watson. When I went to Dr. Watson, he put some drops in my eyes that dilated the pupils. Before I got back to Arlington, my eyes were so dilated I couldn't read the name of the street or the name above the windshield of the bus I was taking unless I got up real close. However, the Lord led me to the right ones, and when I told Mrs. Mosely I had traveled home by guess, she was horrified. She wanted to know why I hadn't told them so someone could have gone with me. Poor Mrs. Mosely, she seemed to fret about my adventurous spirit as much as my mom did.

As I think back, it seems that Cousin Mary had more confidence in my ability to navigate the streets of Washington. At least she didn't act horrified when I told her where I'd been or what I had done. Perhaps it was because she had walked the streets with me to begin with and I was still her "Cousin Ben's daughter." When I took my medical slip in to work, I was given a few additional days off from work to give my eyes time to heal and to pick up my new glasses.

I really enjoyed being out in the country places when night started to come on. After I'd fixed my dinner and eaten, I'd sit on the side porch in the swing and just enjoy the early dusk and watch lightning bugs (fireflies) and children coasting down the hill on roller skates. They and others passing by would wave and speak to me. It was not like in D.C. but was almost like back home. When I resumed work, my coworkers seemed glad to see me back and said they'd missed me. Some of them thought I was sick and wanted to go see me but didn't know where I lived. Eunice and R. C. hadn't come back yet, and I missed them very much. I also missed Sam.

One Sunday evening, I went down the street to see Miss Emmy's girls and found her alone with a fat pretty baby boy, trying to quiet him. A new girl had just moved in. The girl's husband had been sent to Fort Lee, Virginia, which was a good ways out from Washington. He was trying to find a place for her and the baby that would be as close to him as possible, and someone had told him about Miss Emmy's. Although Miss Emmy was filled up, the girls squeezed around and made room for her. She had arrived while Sam was visiting. He and Leroy had seen her one morning when we were getting on the bus to go over to D.C. They'd been impressed with her looks. She was tiny and very pretty. They'd peep at her and then grin at each other all the way over to Washington. I said I was going to tell their mamas that they were trying to flirt with a married woman.

This particular Sunday, I'd been sitting around all day and decided to walk over to Miss Emmy's. All the girls had gone to Fort Myer to visit their boyfriends. The new girl had gone too, but her husband was at Fort Lee. She'd left the baby with Miss Emmy, saying she'd be back real soon. It was now night, and she hadn't returned, and the baby was screaming for all he was worth. I tried to help calm the baby, though I didn't have much experience with babies. "Maybe he's wet," I suggested. He was indeed wet, so we changed his diaper. He hushed for a little bit then the screams resumed. We decided that he was hungry and found his bottle. The bottle had very little milk in it, but he drank it all and wanted more, but there was none. I rocked the baby, and then Miss Emmy rocked him, although her patience was quickly giving out. Her mouth was going, and even though I didn't understand what was being said, from the expression on her face, I could imagine. Time passed, and the baby continued to scream and kick. Another of the girls, Laura, came in. When asked, she said that she didn't know where the baby's mother was. She took him to rock and try to calm him, and I left to go home. The next morning, I was at the bus stop waiting to ride to Cousin Mary's, and there were the mother and baby. So, she'd finally decided to come back! She looked so tiny and frail to be carrying such a hefty-looking baby. We rode over and both got off at Pennsylvania Avenue and then went our separate ways. That was the last any of us ever saw of her or her baby, either one. She never returned to Miss Emmy's, although all of her clothing and the baby's clothing and other belongings were still there. Sometime later, her husband called, but no one knew anything to tell him. I never did learn what became of them. Miss Emmy finally stored all that she'd left in the attic, and that was that—a real-life mystery.

Mrs. Mosely's garden was giving her lots of cucumbers, squash, and other things. She wanted to know if my mom made pickles, and if so, how she made them. I didn't know, but wrote home for Mama's fourteen-day pickle recipe. Miss Mosley then got involved in canning for the summer. I was still meeting new people at work, but Rhoda remained my best buddy. Perhaps it was because of our age that we had a lot in common. She was making plans to enter a teachers' college in the fall and wouldn't be with me much longer. Another young girl I'd met working in a different department was Lillian. Like Rhoda, she enjoyed walking and doing new things. One Sunday she had me meet her at her house. She lived with her sister on a street across the pike. When I got there, she asked if I'd ever walked over the cemetery. I said that I had done some walking there because I'd been to the Tomb of the Unknown Soldier and the Amphitheater. It was a pleasant day, just right for walking. We entered the cemetery through the gate facing our building, which was south, I guess. We wandered about the cemetery reading names, dates, and inscriptions on headstones.

Looking up, we saw that we were near the gate opening toward Memorial Bridge, which leads into D.C. It appeared so close, that we decided to walk to town and get cold drinks. Halfway across the bridge we discovered that it was farther than it looked. Lillian suggested that we stop and take a rest. We sat on a low railing and Lillian took out cigarettes for a smoke, offering one to me.

"Thanks, but I don't smoke," I said.

"Take one anyway," she said. "It will really rest you."

I had tried these things before, and they'd done nothing but made my mouth taste nasty. Maybe this one was different, I thought, so I let her light one for me and started to smoke away. When we stood up to get on with our walk, my head felt light, and I still don't know if it was because I was rested or because I was drunk on cigarette smoke. We made it on past the Lincoln Memorial, then the Reflecting Pool, the Washington Monument, and then on to Pennsylvania Avenue. After we'd had a cold root beer, we headed back the same way we'd come. There was still lots of daylight left when we reached the cemetery. The trees and the green grass were so cool and restful. We sat on a bench and just enjoyed the beauty around us. Again, we started reading inscriptions on headstones, and time passed quickly.

We were reading a verse from "Flanders Field," the one about throwing the torch, when I suddenly remembered something and said, "Lillian, doesn't this place close up at six p.m.?" She didn't know, but I thought I'd seen a sign on the gate the day Sylvia and I had gone to the Tomb, showing what time the gates opened in the morning and closed in the evening. I looked at my watch and saw that it was only a few minutes until six o'clock and we didn't know how far we were from the gate, or even which direction the gate was in. We forgot the soldiers and started running. Since the sun was setting westward, from that, I got my bearings for south. The last thing I wanted was to be locked up in a cemetery full of dead people all night. It turned out that we were closer to the gate than we thought, and we reached it just as the gatekeeper was beginning to close up. Now that was one surprised man to see two scared girls tearing through the graves. We yelled for him to wait, wait, wait! After we had literally shot through, we stopped to catch our breath and say thanks. He laughed and told us that a few more minutes and the gate would have been locked and he'd have been gone.

By now our feet were beginning to make themselves felt and we still had about three more blocks to go. I felt like Peter Rabbit must have felt when he made his escape from Mr. McGregor's garden. When we finally reached home, I was a weary person with very sore feet. Mrs. Mosely was in the kitchen. I smiled and said hi to her and she did the same and then she just waited. She knew me well enough to know that I'd probably been doing something she wouldn't approve of. Finally, I asked if she had a bucket I could soak my feet in. "What's wrong with your feet?" she asked.

"I walked over to Washington and back."

She just gaped at me and said, "Walked to Washington and back?"

"Yes, ma'am."

It was a while before she could digest this news. Then, she asked if I knew it was thirteen miles one way from where we lived to Washington.

"No ma'am, I didn't know that, but my feet feel like it."

"Whatever made you do such a thing? You've walked twenty-six miles. Why didn't you take the bus?"

"My girlfriend and I thought it would be fun to walk."

She mumbled some more, and then she went to the basement for a bucket. After I'd had a bath and put on comfortable night-clothes, I filled the bucket with hot water and then sat in my room to read and soak my sore feet. Most of the girls at work couldn't understand why I enjoyed walking when I could ride the bus or streetcar. One day, I was going home with one girl who lived in northeast Washington, when we had to transfer to another streetcar. The streetcar was a long time coming so, I said, "Let's walk."

"Oh, no, we don't walk like that up here, we have streetcars, buses, and cabs," she told me. She also said I was country to walk so much.

"Yes, I am country, and I like being country." I happened to know she was from the South and from hillbilly country at that.

Work was going well at the office and we still had new ones hired now and then. Rhoda was getting ready to leave us, as she'd be a full-time college student in the fall. I would miss her very much. I'd had so many good times with her. We'd been raised alike. She'd told their family doctor about me, and he was curious about how I lost my hearing so she asked me if I'd go with her on her next checkup and meet him. I agreed. He was an older man, large in stature and pleasant. I felt at home with him and easily answered all of his questions. He tested me with a tuning fork and said he wished he could do something to help me. I said I was fine and not to worry about it and thanked him. I told Rhoda it was very kind of her to be concerned about me, but I was used to being deaf now and I was truly okay.

L. B. (Mrs. Moore) preferred her own food to what was avail-able downstairs and liked to share it with me. Thus, some nights I'd get a drink from a machine and stay upstairs with her while the others went down to the cafe. We talked of Wilmington, our families, work, and of course recipes and cooking. One of our girls was leaving us to join the WACs. After she'd joined and had been issued her uniform, she came back to see us before being sent farther away. She looked very pretty and it was sad to see her leave. Most of the night force had started out together and there was a bond between us. One of the newer girls named Vivian lived with her mother and her two little girls while her husband was in service. One day she didn't come to work or call in sick. Mr. Gaskins called her mom to see what was going on with her. He was told that she had left for work as usual. She never showed up and when he called again the next evening she still had not been home either. We heard that she never returned home, and no one knows what became of her. A tall friendly girl from Kentucky named Ross replaced her.

The summer was nearing an end. One day, while walking, I felt someone run up and grab me from behind. Quickly, I turned around, ready to battle if necessary. It was Cora Lee, one of the girls from school. How glad I was to see her! We hugged and laughed. She'd been on the same streetcar, but didn't see me until I got off. She said she remembered the way I walked. She then pulled the cord for the streetcar to stop, got off and ran to catch up with me. She also said that two other girls had told her they'd been to my Cousin Mary's house to see me when I lived with her, but by the time she got the opportunity to go to the N Street address, I'd moved. She told me where she lived and asked why I didn't come live with her. In her neighborhood, she said, there were lots of deaf people, including a whole bunch from school who lived near her. They had parties and visited each other all the time, and she felt that I might like living there better than living with hearing people. I thanked her, but told her that the people I lived and worked with were fine and that we got along okay.

"Not me, I don't want to live with oral people because they laugh at you and think you are funny," she told me. "We have good times and party."

"That's nice," I said, "and I'm glad you all have good times together." I told her I had a good government job that I liked and that I liked where I lived.

She said she didn't know much about Arlington, only that it was far out in the country and dull. I laughed and told her that perhaps I was also country and probably dull as well. She gave me her address and said for me to come to visit them. We parted with promises to see each other again very soon.

I thought of what she had said about hearing people. It was true that some hearing people would laugh at us or think us crazy, but the ones I lived and worked with treated me extremely well and seemed to accept me as a friend. Deaf people were my world, but so were many hearing people, and I was not going to denounce them and just be with the deaf-Blind people. Other impaired people continued on with their lives, and I was determined that I would and could do the same. People are people, I told myself, and I had learned to take people as I found them. I still follow that practice.

After visiting Laura, I decided to walk up to N Street and see my other family. Cousin Mary said the children had gone around the corner to visit with Uncle George and Agnes at their apartment. I'd forgotten that they had just married and were having a wedding reception. I wasn't dressed but said I'd stop in and congratulate them. The reception was going full swing. They didn't care one bit that I wasn't dressed up and insisted that I stay and make merry with them. I did, and we had a great time. Uncle George looked happier than I'd ever seen him. He'd been married before to a very beautiful woman who had, unfortunately, died in childbirth. The baby died too, and Uncle George had been a heartbroken man. Everybody was glad when he met Agnes and started to live his life again. Agnes seemed to be a very nice person. She worked as an office nurse for the eye doctor I had previously gone to see. It was her first marriage, and she was all rosy and radiant. I was so happy for them. It was beginning to get late, so Leroy and Elnora rode out to Arlington with me to make sure I got home safely.

The war raged on. I've never known the home people to go as all-out in support of our boys and our country in order to try to win this war. Women were taking jobs that had previously been given to men in order to free the men up to join the military. One day I saw a group of women working along the railroad tracks clearing brush and trash. There were other women who drove cabs and buses. My brother's girlfriend, Lucille, was working in a factory in Buffalo. I think her job was to help make airplane parts. There were others who sewed, making parachutes and other necessary items. Any serviceman or woman on a weekend pass who was not able to go home could always find a place to sleep in whatever town or village they happened to be in. They were gladly made welcome in houses where families shared their rationed food with them. Some churches made a practice of serving chicken dinners on certain nights each week, just for service people. Other families would put signs in the windows of their homes saying, "Come in and get a wing and a prayer" after the song "Coming In On a Wing and a Prayer."

My brother Bennie's wife Mable had a younger brother named John C. who was stationed nearby in Maryland. She gave him my address. When he got leave, he came over and took me and one of my friends, Irene, to a movie to see *Lassie Come Home*. I enjoyed the movie, which made me cry and laugh. Afterwards, he treated us to dinner at a restaurant on U Street. We enjoyed our outing with him, especially Irene. She said it was so good to be escorted again out in public by a male. These days men were scarce. Seemingly, the only men who were left were old geezers or young kids. After that, John C. stopped in to see me anytime he was able and would always eat with me. Another frequent visitor during this time was my cousin Norwood Boney, who was Cousin Helen's son. He was stationed at Fort Myers. At the office we were asked to bring in canned food, toilet articles, scented soap, and shaving supplies. The Russians were among our allies and were also having it hard, so we tried to help them too.

I hadn't seen the handsome guard in a while, but one evening I looked up and saw him on patrol in our corridor. Upon passing by, he looked in, saw me, and winked. I looked down at my work and pretended I didn't see him. The next day, after lunch, he walked Pauline, one of the other girls, back to our office. I thought that was great because I believed she was the prettiest girl in our department. Although there were a couple more who were said to be beautiful, Pauline's personality was as pretty as her looks. She had a friendly, breezy way of passing by and giving you a smile and a wink. She reminded me a lot of my Cousin Bert's daughter, Annie Ruth. The guard walked her to the office a few times, and I felt he was in the right hands.

One day, he decided to stop by my desk. I wanted no part of a handsome, flirting male, especially a hearing one. Besides, I had already found the person who I wanted to be with, namely Maleon. He was scheduled to be transferred soon. He'd be in Gunnery School and hoped it would be a lot closer to home so we could see each other more. They were now letting the Black boys into different areas of service. Maleon said he wanted to be a tailgunner on a bomber. To me that sounded scary, but he would be able to make rank and would be a staff sergeant. Whatever, I just hoped he'd come home.

Bennie was still in England. He told me how nice the English people treated him. He had become friends with a family near London who invited him and his friend, Hogan, to their house for weekends. Food was scarce over there too. The Germans were sending bombs across the channel, but the English made the best of it and shared what they had with them. (This was the London Blitz, during 1942–43.) The irony of it was that Bennie and his friend were American boys, fighting for their country, but it was another country that accepted them and treated them as human beings. Bennie also said that the countryside was the most beautiful he'd ever seen. I loved reading his letters, as they were always so interesting, and he'd tell me he was proud of me for being where I was. I cried when he told me that. It made me wish we were back home so I could again follow him as he plowed the fields and listen to him talk, telling me the name of a particular bird that we heard in the woods. Before I became deaf, he taught me to recognize bird calls and other sounds. I read my little biblical testament daily and prayed for all those dear to me, and for our country as well.

It was late August by now, and soon it would be fall. I put in a request to get a week off for Christmas so I could go home. We had to put in our requests for vacation time far in advance. Our work was so essential it had to be kept up with. There was no time off for Thanksgiving, and in order to be off for Christmas Day, we had to work the Sunday before Christmas. I usually walked to work alone, but at night, I would ride home with Mr. Minor and three other girls. There was a two-story wooden house a little way along the street behind the Annex. The Annex had some connection to the house, but I didn't know what it was. Usually a messenger boy was leaving the Annex with some folders heading for the house at about the same time I was on my way to work. This was happening on the backside of the building where I always entered, which was through the post office wing. When the messenger passed me, he'd tip his hat and speak. Being raised by my mama to show my manners, I always answered nice and polite. After a while, I began to wonder why his trips always happened to be at the precise time I passed, so I started to walk on the other side and would cross over only upon reaching the Annex. When I would be just opposite the gate, the messenger boy would still tip his hat and bow his head from across the street. I'd nod and keep going.

One day, he waited until I was almost opposite him and crossed over to my side of the street before I could change direction. I thought, what now? This time he tipped his hat before he reached me, then he smiled and held out a folded piece of paper. I took the paper, wondering what it was, but I kept going. When I reached my desk, I opened the paper and discovered that it was a love letter!!! Mercy do! In the course of his rambling words, he said he lived in D.C. on Fifteenth Street. He also said that he had a large house that was all his own. He gave me the house number and invited me to come over and have dinner with him. He said that I could have whatever my appetite craved. In fact, he closed by saying he'd crawl all the way from China to look at my blue eyes. Ironically, I had never had blue eyes. My goodness gracious, I thought, what ailed the man? I took the letter over to Jones and Irene. They were both indignant. "Some nut trying to pick you up," Jones said, and she doubted that he lived in a large house by himself anywhere, let alone on Fifteenth Street especially as scarce as housing was and people being asked to rent empty space to government workers. Irene agreed, and said that I should carry a stick to whack him with if he got fresh. I said I'd find another way to get to work or would ride the bus, which I did. I've always appreciated the way my coworkers made sure I had a ride in the right direction at quitting time.

As long as I lived in D.C., there was always someone for me to ride home with until I got off the bus, and then I would get the streetcar. However, after the weather became warm, Phyllis and I would walk up Tenth Street together. After she was transferred back to New York, I made the walk alone. Now here in Arlington, it was a different group, consisting of Sylvia, Doris, and her roommate, Choisy, along with our driver, Mr. Minor. They'd tell me to come on and ride with them. One night Choisy and I were walking by ourselves when we got near an overpass and had to stop before crossing the street. A large black car, driven by an older White man, stopped directly in front of us. He told us to get in. We didn't answer, but just stood and stared at him until he drove away. I've often wondered if he thought Choisy was a White girl or what. She was from Trinidad and was quite tall and fair, with red hair and green eyes, but he sure couldn't have mistaken me for a White girl. After that we made sure we had a ride unless the other two girls were with us.

A few people asked me how it felt to be riding with the bosses. I hadn't even thought of them as being bosses. Choisy was a supervisor and so was Doris. Sylvia, I believe, was head typist. Mr. Minor was also up the chain of command somewhere. Of course, Mr. Gaskins was the headman, and Miss Coates was his assistant. I found them all to be just plain, nice and friendly people like the rest, and I did not hesitate to say so. Often, I went across the pike to visit with the girls. Doris and Choisy's landlady looked a lot like my Aunt Mary, tall and straight with white hair. Her name was Mrs. Smith. In addition, some of the women who cleaned our office lived in Arlington, and I was friends with them also. Sometimes they'd start cleaning before closing time. I'd always roll my chair back so they could more easily clean under my desk. Our friendships started with smiles, and before long we exchanged names and talked regularly.

One Sunday Mrs. Moseley asked if I'd like to go to church with the family, and I readily agreed. It was the church I'd previously noticed on a hilltop between where we lived and the cemetery. When we arrived at church, they seated me near the front where I could see Mrs. Moseley and Doretha. It was also where the children sat. Mrs. Moseley was choir director, and Doretha sang in the choir. When the congregation had to stand and sing, I stood too, even though I couldn't sing with them. Some of the kids looked up at me, and one gave me a little nudge, indicating that I should start singing. I smiled down at her and shook my head. Sometime afterwards she asked why I didn't sing? I told her I was deaf and couldn't hear the music. That surprised her but didn't faze her in the least. She spread the word to the other children, and soon all of them knew they had a deaf person in their midst. The child next to me became their spokesperson. She seemed to be about nine years old or perhaps ten. Digging out paper and pencil, she started writing notes. What was my name? Where did I live? Why couldn't I hear? When the service was over and Mrs. Moseley came with some of her friends who she wanted to introduce to me, she shooed all of my new young friends away.

They knew where I lived though and came in a bunch to roller-skate downhill on the side street that ran by the sunroom and the porch where I liked to sit. I was invited to come out and skate with them, but I said I'd better not, thinking about the expression that would be on my landlady's face if she saw me go whizzing by on roller skates.

Having been raised on level farmland of southeastern North Carolina, I found the pretty green hills of Virginia fascinating to look at. I loved to look out the office window late in the evening when the sun was going down behind them. It seemed that purplish haze would cover the hills, and it all looked like a painting. It was amazingly beautiful. Jones noticed me gazing out the window and asked me what I was looking at. When I tried to point out the beauty of it, she said she didn't know I was a poet.

"Me? I'm no poet," I said.

"You sound like it," she replied.

After that, I kept my thoughts to myself. I still enjoyed my view and sitting in the swing on the side porch some evenings, watching it turn dark as the fireflies flitted about.

Looking at the old houses on the street, I could just imagine things as they had been a long time ago when people traveled with horses and carriages or buggies. Walking into the village was also a pleasant experience. The village had a drugstore with a book section. I loved to browse among the books and would usually buy a couple of mysteries such as Ellery Queen, Perry Mason, etc. I also bought a box of chocolates before leaving, and I always visited the bakery. They had the most delicious brownies that were still warm and cost only fifty cents a dozen. One morning I'd just arrived back home with a bag of brownies when Norwood Boney came in. I offered him some of the brownies and a glass of milk. Just as they were all about to disappear, Norwood saw an army jeep pass by. He jumped up, saying that it was his sergeant out looking for him. He was on some sort of detail and while passing by had decided to stop to speak to me. The milk and brownies had made him forget the time; thus he left in a hurry. At least his sergeant saved me a few brownies. Other than my ongoing worry about the war and the people I loved who were involved in it, I was happy with my life. I was happy with my job, my friends, and the things that I did. I knew that one day the war would be over and that the workers would probably no longer be needed. I didn't dwell on that, because I had proven that I could be independent and take care of myself.

It always surprised me how many of my friends, both in and out of the office, seemed to enjoy being with me. There was another girl who asked if I'd like to ride over to the Pentagon with her one Sunday night for dinner. She'd heard that the food was good over there. Her name was Ruth, and she was from South Carolina. She and her husband had both been teachers when he was taken out of the classroom and put in the army. Upset at their separation, and to help her pass the time more quickly, she'd also left and taken a government job here in D.C. The Sunday that we visited the Pentagon was the first time either of us had ever been inside, though we had passed under the building many times. Taking an elevator up to the first floor, we explored as much as we could. We also discovered that it was built around a courtyard. The courtyard was beautiful with tables and chairs, fountains, flowers, etc. People could sit out there for lunch. We found that one of the cafeterias was open and decided to have dinner there. The food was okay, but not as good as the food that we had at the Navy Annex. After dinner, we went on to another floor. I was amazed because it was like being on a city street. Both sides of the corridor were lined with all kinds of shops and stores. There were branches of some of the best-known stores in Washington, including drugstores, jewelry stores, and a bookstore. We browsed around and purchased a few things and then headed for home. It was really awesome being in such an important building where so many important events took place. This was where the girls at Miss Emmy's house worked. My thought was there sure was a lot of space that had to be cleaned. Ruth wasn't with us long after this, so I'm glad we had the opportunity to enjoy this outing together. Ruth's husband came home on leave and spent a few days, and shortly afterwards, she resigned and left. I

think her father took sick and she went home to help him out
with his drugstore.

And so it is, we meet people and form friendships, then before you know it, either they're gone or you have to go. As in
school, my friends were like family to me, and now we were all
miles apart. More of the kids from home had either gone into the
military or had gone up north to work. James Arthur Hayes was
in the navy, and Harding Thompson was in the air force. Even
one of the schoolboys, Lorenzo, had been drafted, and he was
supposedly deaf. It became evident that he could hear well
enough to suit the army. I recalled that when I was in school there
had been blind kids who could see enough to read print. They'd
also discovered a deaf girl who could hear as well as anyone and
thus, she had been sent back home. I guess they must have just
liked being in a deaf and blind school.

# 7

# Changing Times

*Now fades the glimmering landscape on the sight,*
*And all the air a solemn stillness holds,*
*Save where the beetle wheels his droning flight,*
*And drowsy tinklings lull the distant folds;*

Thomas Gray,
"Elegy Written in a Country Churchyard"

BY NOW, it was fall again and my second year out of school. I remembered how beautiful the woods were around Raleigh, those that were behind our campus and also the woods at home, especially out by the pond. I felt lonely for the first time in a good while. I had not been lonely before because I'd been so busy with my work, being with new people and experiencing new things. Now, I thought of the old times, probably because of the particular time of the year. It seems that fall always brings back old memories for me. I spent a lot of time sitting in the porch swing, just thinking, and sometimes I would just sit and try and imagine how it must have had looked around Arlington before the Civil War. There must have been kids out playing with tom walkers (stilts) and rolling hoops instead of bikes and roller skates; then, there would have been the women in long full dresses and wearing bonnets, sitting on the porches of these old houses or on the streets. The men would have been on horseback or riding in buggies. I had read the book *Gone with the Wind*, and now here I was living among the houses that had been built so long ago. It was so easy for me to see it as it must have been back then.

Although the homes on this side of the pike were old, they were all in good repair and had all the modern conveniences like plumbing and electricity. Across the pike many of the houses were new, mostly brick. It was so nice and comfortable living at Miss Moseley's house. Every Friday night when I came home from work, there was a pile of freshly ironed, sweet-smelling bed linen at the foot of my bed. I could go to the basement and wash any of my personal things in her washing machine and was also able to iron them. I felt so much at home that I took to doing little things for her. I would mop the kitchen floor every Wednesday. Back then, we had milk delivered in glass bottles, and I would bring in the milk from the front porch where the milkman would leave it. We would order two or three quarts a week. The cream was a few inches deep at the top, and it could be skimmed off or shaken up and blended with the rest of the milk. Usually, I would skim off most of mine and give it to Mrs. Moseley to use for cooking or in coffee.

For a while, I really did not have a desire to go anyplace except to work and to the village to buy groceries. If the days were nice, I'd sit in the swing reading a mystery story or would sometimes just sit there doing nothing. On cool rainy days, I loved to put on an old bathrobe and would sit on a hassock by the radiator in my room eating chocolates while I read, or until time to get dressed to work. The weather was turning nippy, and like North Carolina, the trees were something beautiful to look at. It seemed unreal at times, looking at hills in the distance with such beautiful colors. Mrs. Moseley was gathering in the last of her garden, squash, cucumbers, tomatoes, etc., and was trying to decide what dishes to make with them.

The neighborhood on the other side of the street and up Columbia Pike was called Green Valley. I had the address of Mrs. Annie Hayes's sister who lived over there. Mama kept asking if I'd looked her up yet, so one Sunday evening I decided I'd like to go for a walk. Dot, one of the girls across the street, said she'd go with me. We started from the northern end of Green Valley early in the afternoon. It was necessary for us to ask about how to find the address that we were looking for. Finally, we found the street and found that it ran south. We walked south, checking the numbers on the houses as we went. The houses got fewer and farther apart and it had also started to get late in the evening. I was determined that since I'd come this far, that I was going to find that house. The street we were now on ran through a forest with even fewer houses. It was really a green valley, but was very quiet and pleasant. Then suddenly, the street curved and went around in a different direction, and there, just a short distance away, was the house we sought. The only problem now was that no one was at home. Oh well, it was too late to visit anyway. We saw a sign saying Columbia Pike right up ahead. As it turned out, we'd walked past the Village and were quite a ways from home. When we did finally reach our places of abode, it was dark. I have no idea how many miles I walked that day.

The front yard of of the Spanish-style house next door was fenced in, with a beautiful rosebush in the corner nearest the house. I loved to look down on that bush from my window. Now that it was fall and turning cold, all the roses had fallen off one by one until only one large rose was left. I took to watching that rose to see how long it would bloom all alone. Every morning I'd go to the window and raise the shade to see if it was still there. The blossom would be as fresh and pretty as ever. Sometimes I'd even go look at it through the fence. It was even prettier close up. I'd pass it on my way to work. It was like the song "The Last Rose of Summer." For some reason, that rose stayed there for the longest time, until finally one morning after a heavy frost, I saw that all the petals had fallen off.

The civil rights movement had not yet started at this time, but I think that things were beginning to stir in that direction. I started reading more about the NAACP, and one Sunday afternoon, Doretha asked me if I'd like to ride with her to attend a meeting that was being held in Green Valley. We went to the meeting, but there weren't enough people to hold a meeting, so we returned home. At least I didn't have to wear my feet out this time as I had done so many times in the past.

There was a girl who worked at the Annex and rode the bus to and from Washington. One night, she sat in a front seat on the bus and refused to move toward the back when she was asked to do so. The bus driver called the police and had her arrested. It seemed that it was okay to sit closer to the front of the bus as long as you were riding in Washington, but once on the Virginia side of the bridge, all Blacks were required to ride in the back of the bus. Someone had taken up the plight of assisting the girl in straightening this situation out. I guess in the end, she came out okay, because I continued to see her coming and going. On another night, a bunch of White marines boarded the bus that we rode on before I moved to Arlington. I was sitting midway the bus, but one of them plopped down beside me. As usual, I was looking out the window at the night lights shining on the water and different things. I paid him no mind, but when the bus stopped at Pennsylvania Avenue and everybody stood up to get off, the marine wouldn't stand. He continued to sit there with his legs blocking my way and looking at me.

I said, "Excuse me."

I didn't see him say anything, but he just kept looking at me. Looking around, I saw that some of my friends had noticed what was happening and were watching me with concern. I waited a little while longer, then stepped across his legs and got off the bus. Some of the girls said he'd been drinking. I realized that I had been in what could have been a dangerous situation, but again, the Lord was with me, and I came through it just fine.

It was near the end of October when Sylvia and I decided to ride over to Fort Myer along with Miss Emmy's girls and attend Vesper Services one Sunday evening. It was a nice program that was similar to the ones we had in chapel at school. The only difference was that they didn't have anyone signing songs. The service was conducted by a chaplain, and afterwards, we could play games, table tennis, checkers, cards or have refreshments and dance. We enjoyed Vespers, then enjoyed playing games for a while. When we tired of the games, everybody went to the far end of the room where there was a jukebox. Some couples began dancing. I'd met a few of the boys before but didn't want to dance.

One of them laid his cap on my lap and asked if I'd hold it for him because the bib of the cap got in his way. "Sure," I said, and he returned to his dancing.

I loved to watch people dance and was enjoying it when I noticed a woman who'd just come into the room. She was standing in the doorway glaring in my direction. I didn't think it was possible that it was me she was mad at, as I'd never seen her before in my life. However, upon looking around, I saw that there was no one else for her to glare at except me. The boy whose cap I held also saw her and abruptly quit dancing and went to where she was. They appeared to be involved in an argument. He then walked over, picked up his cap, thanked me, put it on his head, went back and started to dance with the woman. Maggie came over and told me it was some woman who claimed him for a boy-friend and was very jealous of him. She'd seen me holding his cap (she recognized the cap), and had then gone on the warpath. At 9:00 pm. it was "get out and go home time." We went to the bus stop, where there was a crowd of guys bidding their girl-friends and wives goodnight. There was lots of hugging and kiss-ing going on. Two of the guys had walked with me and Sylvia to the bus stop. When the bus came and we started to get on, one of the guys asked Sylvia if he could kiss her goodnight. She shook her head and shuddered. I laughed and teased her all the way home.

Fall had really arrived by now, and it was Halloween week already. I remember thinking how cold for it to only be October. I had to use one of my shoe coupons to get warmer leather shoes for the winter. We'd all been wearing sandals and canvas shoes through spring and summer because we were giving all we could in support of our boys. I was still writing to all the guys I had been asked to write, and they still wrote me in return. The young guys were always eager to keep up with what all was happening back home, like the latest shows, songs, and dances. What I didn't learn from the movies and from magazines, I would ask Leroy and Elnora. Most of the popular songs had lyrics that pertained to the war. The songs "The White Cliffs of Dover," "When the Lights Go on Again," and "Yes Indeed," were still going strong.

I first learned of the last song during my final year in school. The father of one of the girls was a preacher. She said someone near them had opened a juke joint. I believe it was located on the same street. Of course, being a preacher, her dad had been tremendously upset. One night while her dad was having family prayer and was praying about the war, asking God not to let any bombs fall on us, in the midst of his prayer someone started the jukebox. The record that was playing at the time was blasting out the words "You'll holler when it hits you, yes indeed." She said her poor father leapt to his feet shouting and shaking his fist. It took a while to calm him down. Additionally some of the words to this song were "You'll holler when it hits you, yes indeed. It comes out if it's in you, yes indeed. Make you shout, Jack it sends you, yes indeed. When that spirit moves you, you'll holler halle-lujah. You'll holler when it hits you, yes indeed." I remember being in a joint at home, and I could always tell when that record was starting up because people would immediately quit talking. The men would push their hats further down on their heads to make sure they didn't lose them during what was going to come next. They'd then grab the hand of the nearest female and cut loose dancing. The entire room would be jumping and swinging at the same time. There were times when I would dance, but most often than not, I'd find a safe place out of the way of those dancing feet and would just watch the others. It was something to see. If there was someone who could not find a partner, no problem, they danced by themselves.

The dancing wasn't anything like what they call dancing now. At that time, dancing was clean, and some of the popular dances were the Big Apple, Trucking, the Susie Q, and the Jitterbug. Nonetheless, the Hays office censored our movies, and also some of the dancing. The Hays office was an organization in Hollywood that reviewed all the movies and dancing and banned or cut parts out they they thought were offensive. One dance called the Duck was banned, and you had to pay a fine if you were caught doing this dance in public. The guys also wanted to know about Frank Sinatra when they would write. They referred to him as that "half-starved-looking little fellow." I told them that I'd seen him pass by in a parade, but knew nothing about his singing, except that the girls and young women screamed and fainted when they went to hear him in person and would also try to tear his clothes off in order to have a piece of his clothing. At that time, Sinatra's most popular song was "That Old Black Magic." More and more Black stars were beginning to come out now. Duke Ellington, Louis Armstrong, Fats Waller, Lena Horne, and Hazel Scott were a few. I wrote to the guys about these rising stars and sent them newspaper and magazine clippings. They wrote to me about the stars that visited their camps. The one they seemed to enjoy the most was Dinah Shore. They said that she was such a nice friendly person.

They also liked to get pictures of home, just everyday homey pictures. It seemed like every young man between eighteen and thirty-five was being drafted. It was said that for a new private enlistee, the pay was twenty-one dollars a month plus food, clothes, and medicine. Somebody came up with a song, "Twenty-One Dollars a Day Once a Month." No one ever told me that that, in fact, was the pay they received, and I never asked. Quite a few of the guys sent me little gifts. They sent pillow tops with the name of their company and their camp, as well as trinkets, picture postcards, and pictures of themselves. My brother Bennie sent me and Eunice beautiful hand-crocheted gloves and perfume from Paris. Willie sent us silver bracelets from Mexico. Anytime I found out which hometown boys where in the navy, I kept a lookout for their names and what they were doing. I found several names I knew who were at Great Lakes Training School in Illinois. My cousin Lionel, I found, was in Miami, Florida. Not too many Blacks were in the navy or in the marines at this time. Most of the Blacks went into the army or the air force.

Maleon's brother Paris was training at Tuskegee, Alabama, to become a pilot. Oftentimes he wrote to me and would call me his "little sister." There were four boys in Maleon's family, but no girls. Maleon was the oldest, and Paris was the second-oldest. The two younger boys were still in school. Paris sent me a picture of himself in his flying outfit, and I saw that he was really handsome. All the girls oohed and aahed over the picture when I would show it to them. The government had finally agreed to let Black boys train to fly, but they were in an all-Black company. It was a long while before we knew that they were flying missions against the enemy with great success. This group of pilots became known as the Tuskegee Airmen. It was years later before we knew anything about the Redtail Angels, as one squadron was known, and about how they fought in North Africa. We did, however, know of Benjamin O. Davis, who was the highest ranking Black soldier at the time. I was proud of anyone who was fighting for our country, but there was a certain pride in knowing that our very own race was proving they could fight just as well as anyone else.

None of my deaf friends ever came out to Arlington to see me. They said I was too far out in the country. While I was at Cousin Mary's, my friend Frances from school would stop in to see me often. One day she was with me upstairs telling me about their latest party and how she had danced. She got up and started showing me how she could do a new step called the Sand and some other new dances. While she was dancing, Uncle George was passing the door and stopped to watch. Later, after she'd gone, he was telling the rest of the family how good my friend could dance and wanted to know who she was. When I told them that she was a friend from school and he realized she was deaf, he just stood there totally surprised. He was even more amazed when I told him that most of the other kids could dance just as well and some of them even better.

The family was also impressed with Thomasina, who they thought was very nice and sensible and also very pretty. One of Thomasina's daughters grew up and became a member of a group of singers known as "Sweet Honey in the Rock." She signs every song that they sing so that her mom can enjoy the songs too. One night at the office after we had signed out, the group that I rode home with every night was going down, using the stairs. Somehow, Doris tripped a few steps from the bottom and fell. Her knee started swelling at once, so instead of going home, we carried her over to Washington. The doctor put her to bed, as her knee was sprung, or perhaps it may have even been fractured. She was at home for a good while and we missed her terribly. Then, one Monday, Laura came in and was all smiles. A wedding ring had been added to the engagement ring that she'd been wearing. Her groom was a sailor. They had only been able to spend a weekend together, and he was already gone. She was still happy though, and we were all glad for her. Rhoda was in Teachers College now, and I no longer saw her. I missed her very much.

Another girl who lived in northeast Washington invited me to dinner at her home one Sunday. Her name was Roots. Her mom was away, so she cooked and served dinner. At her house was her father, a younger sister, a brother, and the family dog. She'd had a few books of poetry published, and I enjoyed reading it. It turned out to be a very pleasant Sunday. She saw me to Pennsylvania Avenue when I was ready to leave. I thought again of how my school friends had warned me about hearing people, and I understood how they felt. I loved them for their concern, but I just had to be my own person and take everybody as I found them whether blind, deaf, Black, White, or whatever. It was their attitudes and their hearts that mattered most. I know that I'm deaf and that I'm no different from other deaf people. However, I recognize real friendship when it's offered to me.

Cold weather had now set in, so I didn't ramble quite as much. Sylvia and the people she lived with invited me to come over to play whist, a popular card game of the time with them one evening. It was not yet dark when I went and it was my intent to be home by night, but we were having so much fun that time

passed quickly, and soon it was dark. Just as I told them I had to
go, there came a loud banging on the front door. It was the air
raid warden telling us to put out every light. We wanted to finish the card game we had going, so after the blinds and curtains
were closed and all lights were out except one near the table, we
continued our game, thinking that no light was visible to the
outside. Wrong! We'd only been playing a few minutes when the
banging started again, and the girls said that this time the warden
had threatened us with a fine; at that point, we decided to call it
quits for the night.

There was another girl who lived down the street, and she
said she was on her way home when I told her I, too, was heading home. We had no way of knowing how long the blackout
would last. It was a cold night with bright moonlight. After the
other girl reached her house, I was within sight of Columbia
Pike, which was just ahead of me. I saw a man who was walking a ways behind me. My feet picked up speed, and I kept
looking back, hoping that he would turn off someplace. No such
luck! He seemed to be walking faster too. I started to trot or jog
and soon crossed the Pike that put me about a block from my
home, but here the houses were farther apart. My heart was
thumping by now, and he was still behind me, so I ran the rest
of the way. After letting myself in the house, I went upstairs,
took off my coat, then went back down to the kitchen for a
snack. I was still thanking the good Lord for getting me home
safe and sound. Mrs. Moseley and her son were also in the
kitchen. He had just arrived home and still had on his hat and
overcoat. I stared closely at him and his clothing. The hat was
the same shape as the one belonging to the man who had been
behind me. Sure enough, he'd told his mother that he had been
on his way home and saw me ahead of him and had tried to
catch up with me to accompany me home so I wouldn't be

afraid. He said he never knew that I could move so fast. We had a good laugh about the incident. I was glad it turned out to be Andrew and not some stranger that I would have to be afraid of in the future. It's still difficult for some people to believe that I actually walked the streets of Washington, D.C., and Arlington, Virginia, alone both day and night. I have been told that cops with partners now patrol the areas where I once walked and that the cops also have police dogs with them on patrol. God was surely with me then and is with me now.

Doris was almost ready to be discharged from the hospital so Sylvia and I went to the hospital to bring her home. We rode over by bus. Her leg was still in a heavy cast, so we got a cab to carry us back to Arlington. With support from the two of us, as well as the use of crutches, she managed to get upstairs and settled in her room. It was good having Doris back with us, as she was always a lot of fun. One morning I went over to her place, and she and Choisy, her roommate, were still in bed. It was a cold morning, and both of them had on flannel pajamas, robes, heavy socks, and long woolen scarves over their heads and around their necks. I asked them if they were going someplace, and they said no, that their room was freezing. Mrs. Smith didn't have any heat in the house. It was a lovely brick house, but she didn't like to spend her money on gas or coal for the furnace. They asked me how my room was, and I told them that my room was old-fashioned but clean and warm. They advised me that I should hang on to the room if it was warm. Their rooms were up-to-date but were as cold as ice. They asked their landlady every day if she would please get the heat started up. She would promise them faithfully that she would, but every night when they arrived home, they found it was still like ice. Even the portable electric heater they bought didn't help very much. They began to look for another room to rent.

One night I dropped my door keys as I was getting out of the car, but I didn't realize I had dropped them until I got to the door, so Mrs. Moseley had to open the door for me. The next day Mr. Minor held the keys up and wanted to know who they belonged to. He said that his wife had found them in the car. When I answered that they were my keys, Doris told him she was going to tell his wife that the keys came from the Logan Circle Hotel near Thirteenth Street and that his girlfriend left them in his car. The Logan Circle Hotel was a small hotel that was rumored to be a brothel, or house of prostitution. We had a lot of fun teasing him about this. Doris and Choisy finally found another room to rent that had heat, but it was in D.C. They hated to move over to the city but found it necessary. After they moved, we missed them very much.

Now that the days were short and cold, I stuck close to home. I was still happy reading my mystery stories and writing to the boys. The "special" boys that I enjoyed writing to the most were, of course, Maleon, my two brothers, and Mickey. Mickey was my buddy. He was stationed in Trinidad, and his letters were full of funny things that happened in camp, and he talked about the people in that country and about his friends, etc. Maleon wrote me sweet letters in which he would tell me about his favorite songs, and through our correspondence we discovered that we both loved poetry. Back then couples liked to choose a theme song of their very own. Maleon chose "In the Blue of Evening" as our song. After this, I was in my room one morning and became acutely aware that I was hearing what sounded like music. I knew that this could not possibly be the case. Doretha's room was next to mine, but I had never before heard anything from the direction of her room and also, she had already left for work. Andrew's room was across the stair landing, and he was also at work. Thinking it had to be my imagination, I went on about my business, but the sound persisted. I stood, still concentrating on the sound, and it became obvious that it was in fact *music*, and that it was coming from downstairs! I flew down the stairs, and sure enough, Mrs. Moseley was at her piano practicing some church songs. She stopped to ask me if anything was wrong.

I said, "Oh, no, I just heard your music."

Her mouth fell open. "How?" she asked.

"I don't know, but I did and I came down to see if I was really hearing music." She was delighted and started to play another song, "Hide My Soul," and she truly went to town on it. After that I would buy the sheet music for all the songs Maleon said he liked and would get her to play them for me. If it wasn't one of my good days, she'd play anyway, and I'd stand close by the piano and catch the vibrations. I asked her if she thought I'd be able to learn to play. She didn't think so because I would need to be able to hear notes really well. No matter, I still enjoyed my newfound pleasure, and Maleon said he would play them for me. He was majoring in music, and wanted to become a music teacher in a school.

There were times when I would stop to think about all the good things that had come my way during my lifetime. Some of the things that had happened were hard to believe after listening to so many negative comments from my deaf friends about the hearing world. I would go over my thoughts again and again. I was in a good job that enabled me to pay all of my living expenses and to help my parents financially. I was also out among hearing people that I had never met before, but had been totally accepted and was getting long as well as any of the others. I had a supportive family at home, plus Cousin Mary and her family. I even had a clean decent place to live and was proud for friends to visit me at home. During that time, Washington was packed with people who were either in service or who were doing government work. There was an extreme shortage of living space, and some people lived wherever they could find a place to lie down. I even saw people sleeping on park benches after I got off work at night. At the very top of all of the good things that had happened to me, I had found someone who cared for me and who shared all of the same dreams and hopes that I had. With Maleon there was no need for me to hear, as we thought alike. Even with his good looks, his background, his religion, and all, he cared about me for who I was. My family liked him a lot, and I felt completely at home with his family. It amazed me to remember that I had tried to run him off in the beginning. When I thought about all of my wonderful blessings, I wanted to tell any other deaf person who felt that they couldn't live with the hearing that if I could do it, then they could too.

Now, at the time when I am writing this, I keep up with deaf happenings by reading the *Silent News* and other newspapers and magazines. I see where so many deaf individuals have wonderful professional jobs and careers—they travel and win awards, along with a long list of other achievements. I am so happy for them and proud of them. Back then, during the 1940s and 1950s, Black deaf people were not given these wonderful opportunities. They stuck together mostly because they understood each other and felt more secure with one another. I've had only one deaf friend that I met since my school days, and she is not someone I grew up with. She lost her hearing at age twelve or thirteen and still has speech. Her family was reluctant to openly recognize her deafness. She was sent on to public school and never learned a single sign. She later married a hearing man and raised a family of girls and boys who all turned out to be great individuals. For some reason she never became reconciled with being deaf. It just grieved her that she couldn't hear, and she never gave up trying anything that might restore her hearing. She died several years ago, and I still miss corresponding with her. I think we all have to make our own choices. I surely made mine, and even after all these years, I am still fully content with my decisions. Yes, God has truly blessed me.

# 8

# Home for the Holidays

*Yet the beauties that I loved*
*Are in my memory,*
*I spit into the face of time*
*That has transfigured me.*

W. B. Yeats,
"The Lamentations"

MY REQUEST for leave to go home for the holidays had been granted. Once again I took to the streets of Washington in search of gifts for my folks. I'd read an advertisement in an outdoor magazine where some dog breeders in Pennsylvania were selling AKC, or purebred, dogs of different breeds. I thought of Papa and how he had given me my dog Queen to keep me company while all the other kids were in school. He had then worked at night in order for me to keep the dog when he could have sold her to help ease his financial burden. I had kept Queen until I graduated from high school. Now this was an opportunity for me to sort of repay him, so I ordered an English setter to be shipped to him for his Christmas gift. Next I shopped for the boys, Maleon,

Bennie, Willie, Mickey, Elmer, and Richard, as well as some of those who were still across the ocean. Finally, I had to buy gifts for Mom and the rest of the family. With all this done, I shopped for things to put in the boxes that the office staff was putting together to send to our own boys for Christmas.

There were not many choices for the things that were to be shipped—hard candy, gum, shaving stuff, candied fruit, cigarettes, and stationery were about all. I also decided to treat myself to a new winter outfit for my own Christmas. In one shop, I found a beautiful cream and brown plaid dress made out of real soft wool, and later I found the perfect coat and hat to match the dress. Both were cream-colored, and I bought a pair of brown shoes and a purse. It all added up to more than I had ever paid for clothes in the past. The way I figured, I was earning my own money now and could choose to spend my money as I desired. While trying on dresses, I noticed for the first time that my dress size had changed. I no longer looked round and chubby but instead wore a size five. Some of the freckles on my face had also faded. Oh well, people often change, so it was no big deal. Sylvia was planning to go home to New York for the holidays. With my shopping done, I settled back to wait for time to leave for my trip home. I'd missed out on being home for so many Christmases. I felt the same excitement for the coming holidays that I had as a child. Sylvia was leaving for New York on Sunday night after work.

There was the usual excitement before the Christmas holidays, but there was something different about this year, a heightened sense of worry and fear. The blackouts were happening more frequently now. There were some places that couldn't be lit up at all, the same as in the past year. More of our boys were being wounded, missing in action, and worst of all, being killed. The Germans were bombing London, and France had surrendered. The United States, England, and Russia were fighting as hard as they could, as was China. It seemed that the whole United States, and especially Washington, was in a frenzy of activity. Big Hollywood stars were busy putting on shows to raise money. I bought two newspapers daily to keep up with everything that was happening. Our factories had changed from making domestic things to making anything and everything that they could for the war. Down home, my brother Frank was helping build warships at the Wilmington Shipyard. Bennie had also worked there before he was sent out to fight. My brother Willie's girlfriend was helping build airplanes in New York. She worked at Curtis Wright's as a riveter. The men who were not in the military or building and making something were busy raising food. Women and children were just as busy. It seemed that when they weren't working, they were dancing and partying. I believe that they did this to try to keep from thinking about the war. I also heard that some girls were either getting engaged or actually marrying as many boys as asked them to. They would marry one boy, and when he was shipped out, they would cry for a brief period and then marry another boy without getting a divorce. They were recipients of a stack of allotment checks. I knew one girl, a cousin, who had engagement rings up to her knuckle. Some of these girls were caught receiving multiple checks and ended up in big trouble.

One Friday night I went with Elnora to her hairdresser's house to get her hair done. When we arrived, the living room was packed with soldiers who were dancing, eating, and having a ball. We had to push our way through the crowd to get to the back. With all of this activity going on, some of the office girls, especially those from further up north, in New York and New Jersey, still complained of how dull Washington was, and put in to be transferred back home. My thinking was that if this was dull, I surely didn't want to see any livelier times. We had to work that particular night, so that no one would need to come into the office on

Christmas Day. Since my plans were to leave the next day, I went over to see Sylvia on Sunday morning. She asked me to stay for lunch. I accepted, and she fixed lamb chops, peas, and carrots, and chocolate pudding for dessert. We decided to go on to work from her house. After we had washed the dishes, got her bag ready, and started to leave the house, she told me to wait because she had forgotten something. She ran back into the kitchen, and as it turned out, the item she had forgotten was a stick of "real butter." During that time, real butter was so hard to come by that she felt she couldn't leave it to go to waste or for her landlady to use. She wrapped it in her white napkin and tucked it into her handbag. When we arrived at the office, she placed the butter on a windowsill to keep it from becoming soft. No one seemed to think it strange for anyone to be carrying a stick of butter in their handbag. So much of our food was still rationed and was hard to get that items like real butter were a luxury.

I rode the bus home this time, and when we stopped in Raleigh, I was watching the passersby when I caught sight of someone signing. It was a bunch of the kids from my old school who were also on their way home for Christmas. I was so happy to see them, and I tried to get their attention. One girl, Ella Boyd, saw me and waved. She told the other girl, "I see Herring," but Mrs. King was herding them onto their bus, and we didn't get a chance to talk, or rather to *sign*. When I arrived in Wallace, there was no one at the bus station to meet me. However, another girl from out my way had also come in on the same bus. Mr. Draughn had his cab there so we hired him to drive us to our respective destinations. He was one of our high school teachers, and he drove a taxi on the side. About halfway out of town, he had a flat tire on the cab and had to pull over to fix it. Sarah and I sat back and chatted until he got it fixed. At the time of the flat tire, she was within walking distance of her house, but I had a few more miles to go. The charge for the cab was a mere fifty cents. How good it was to drive up in the yard and be home for Christmas. Someone had been planning to meet me, but there had been a mix-up in the time. No matter, I was home and had arrived in time to help decorate, shop, and bake cakes. That was the part that I loved best.

There were still no electric lights out in the country, but everyone went all-out for holiday decorations. Trees were hung with shiny balls, tinsel, and angel hair. Red bells or wreaths hung in every window. Small branches of holly with bright red berries hung on pictures, doors, or wherever someone wanted to place them. Papa's dog hadn't arrived yet. He knew that the dog had been ordered and was in a tizzy to see him. My niece Maxine was a pretty little toddler who was three years old. She called all of us "Ma." Her eyes were big and bright with the wonder of Christmas and with anticipation of what Santa would bring to her. Once again the house was filled with the special smells of the season. There was the magnificent scent of apples and oranges, the smell of freshly baked cakes and pies, and cedar or pine scent from the Christmas tree, and over it all, you caught the scent of hardwood smoke.

There really is no other time like Christmas. It was mysterious, since nobody knew what they were going to get. But we were ever reminded of the true meaning of the holiday, that is, the birth of our Savior. I could just picture in my mind the shepherds huddled around the fire in a field someplace, trying to get warm, the sky that must have been full of stars, and then the shepherds looking up and seeing those angels over them singing. I wonder what I would have done had I been there during that time. It is most likely that I would have sought out Mama's apron to hide under.

And finally, after much anticipation, the great day was here, which began with opening gifts and then gathering around the breakfast table for fresh sausage, bacon, hot biscuits, and eggs. Also, we would sample some of the cakes that had been made. This particular year, there was a distinct difference. Bennie and Willie were off in the army, and war was raging overseas. Disheartening news continued to be broadcast over the radio and written up in the newspapers. During this time, there was no television to show the actual fighting, bombing, and killing, and perhaps, when I think about it, that was a blessing in itself.

When I went out socializing with Eunice, it was like Washington, the people seemed in a frenzy of trying to forget the war for a little while. They would just dance and party in an attempt to be happy as in the old days. The jukeboxes boomed and blared, flashing their bright lights; the girls laughed and danced even harder; and in between, some of the men would disappear behind the building or down a path for a quick swig of white lightning, or whatever they called their bootleg whiskey at that time. They'd swagger back into the building, fortified and ready for another round of dancing. Some of the women's feet would actually leave the floor while being whirled around. They'd keep up this pace until the place closed for the night, at which time they would stagger out completely exhausted. Some of the girls' shoe heels would look tired too, as they would have become bent under, toward the front of the shoe.

With Christmas over, things settled back into the old routine. A notice came that Papa's dog would be coming in on the next morning train. Sam and I went with him to meet the dog. We arrived a bit early, so Papa parked the truck in a lot next to old Dr. Robinson's office. He then went to attend to some business elsewhere. Sam and I sat in the truck waiting for the train. All of a sudden, an old black pickup truck driven by a White man came racing up and stopped beside us. When he opened the door to get out, he fell out instead. People came running and carried him into Dr. Robinson's office, and a short time later an ambulance came rushing up. Sam and I got out of Papa's truck and went to see what was happening. When the stricken man was brought out on a stretcher to be put into the ambulance, we saw that it was a man we knew. His name was Stedman, and he lived out in the country near us. It seemed that to earn money, he went around to different places buying furs from trappers. Not far out from town, two young men had tried to rob him. He had resisted the robbery attempt and had been shot in the abdomen. His face was so white that he appeared to be dead, and he did die shortly thereafter. Papa's dog finally arrived. It was a pretty young male English setter that was white with black spots. Papa was so proud of him and said he could tell right away that he was smart and a pure breed. He lost no time getting the dog home so he could free him from the crate and try him out.

Now the holidays were over, and I was back at work. I'd found a stack of letters and Christmas cards from the service boys. Maleon had sent me a cameo necklace and some candy. One boy had sent me a whole case of oranges from Florida. Most of them had spoiled by the time I returned, even though Mrs. Moseley had tried to save them. As a rule, January is a dreary month, and this January was no exception. It seemed that the days were darker and longer, or maybe it was because we were finding more and more distressing news in our reports. One day I was checking the muster roll of one ship and discovered that many of the boys were listed as killed. It made me cry as I thought of how their families were waiting for them to one day walk back in the door and be home again. Some of the boys I had been writing to had stopped writing. After sending a card or two to them, I crossed them off and never knew whether they'd been killed in action or just discharged and gone back home and had no need to get mail anymore. I never made any attempt to find out.

The month of January dragged on and was mostly rainy and icy. One morning I slipped on some ice, and Mrs. Moseley sent me to see a neighborhood doctor, whose office was just out on the pike. I never even realized before that there was a doctor near us. His office was in his home, which was a pleasant two-story house just two doors from Mrs. Smith's, where Doris and Choisy used to live. She told me to just ask for Dr. Willacy and tell him that she sent me. I rang the doorbell, and a nice-looking young Black man opened the door. I told him that I was there to see Dr. Willacy. He smiled and said, "That's me." I was completely surprised, as all the doctors I'd been to before were either middle-aged or old White doctors. He showed me into his office, and I told him that I had fallen on the ice and wanted him to check my wrist, I mentioned that Mrs. Moseley had sent me to him. He knew her and asked if I was a relative. After explaining who I was, like most people, especially doctors, he was interested in knowing how or why I had become deaf. I told him what little I knew. He told me he was from Jamaica. He came to this country to study medicine and hadn't been back to his home for fourteen years. As it turns out, my wrist wasn't broken, only sprained a little. He put it under a warm light for a while and then bound it with tape. His fee for his services was three dollars. He continued to be my doctor for as long as I lived in that area. Finally, at long last, February rolled around.

One day while at work, we were all told to report to a room that was located on another floor. All personnel had to have x-rays taken to be screened for tuberculosis. It reminded me of my school days. In one room, we had to strip to our waist and put on large paper bags with holes cut for our head and arms. After this was done, we went into another room to stand before a machine. Some of the employees were not pleased with what was happening and grumbled for a while. Since I had been through a very similar process every year at the school for the deaf, I didn't mind at all. Evidently, everyone's test was negative, because things went on with the same routine as before.

Valentine's Day was approaching, and I started finding Valentine cards in my mail when I came home at night, as well as boxes of candy. Like most young girls, I found this attention thrilling, and it also meant that I had lots of candy to eat while reading my mystery stories. Emma came back to pay us another visit, and she really looked nifty in her Women's Auxiliary Army Corps (WAAC) uniform. I think that if I'd been able to hear, I would have joined too.

I asked Mama how Papa and Prince, his new dog, were getting along. The answer was that they were doing great. Papa said that Prince was one of the smartest dogs he'd ever owned. I thought of Queen, who had been my childhood companion and who had been largely responsible for keeping me from being lonely so much of the time. I also thought about some of the other dogs that had once roamed our yard that I'd loved. There had been one named Joe, and then there was Dinah. They were both coonhounds. Joe was black and white with touches of tan, and he was both loyal and protective of all the family. Dinah, on the other hand, was mostly black with a little white and tan. She was friendly and gentle. They were both sturdy and sleek dogs. We'd had them for so long that they seemed like members of the family.

Eventually they both died. Someone poisoned Joe, and Dinah was just sick. Sam and I attended both of their funerals. First, Papa sewed them up in clean cotton sacks and then loaded them on a wheelbarrow with a shovel and headed for his dog cemetery. Sam and I followed, each with a bouquet of flowers from Mama's flowerbeds that contained zinnia, marigolds, and batchelor buttons. I always cried during these times, but Sam would only frown. I suspect now that he did this in an attempt to keep from crying. As the funeral procession passed the house, Mama would be standing at the end of the porch watching us go by. After digging the grave, Papa would pick up the dog and carefully place it in, then he would start shoveling the dirt back in. When he was done, Sam and I would place our flowers on top of the grave and follow our papa back to the house with the empty wheelbarrow. Except for my sniffing, there was total silence during the burial, as no one felt like talking. However, I secretly said a prayer and tried to picture the dog running happily about wherever it is that dogs go when they die.

February passed, and we slipped into March. One day members of the office staff were given W-2 forms and told to go to a downstairs room where someone would assist us in filing our taxes if we didn't want to try to do it ourselves. Taxes were due to be filed not later than the fifteenth of March. I had read about income taxes here and there but had never had any dealings with them personally since I had never earned enough money to file. One evening I asked to be excused and went downstairs to get my taxes done. The lady who did the preparations for me was very nice and explained everything that she did. I came away with papers saying that I had to go to the post office and buy a money order for a little over a hundred dollars and mail it to the Internal Revenue Service. That was my introduction to income tax returns. On the day I mailed the papers to the IRS, I left the post office with only nineteen cents and some streetcar tokens in my handbag. Fortunately, I would be getting another check a day or two later. I didn't have to pay carfare to get to work and could carry lunch until I got paid again.

Not long after this, I had arrived home and was eating a snack and opening my mail when Mrs. Moseley came up the stairs and motioned for me to come to where she was. I went to the top of the stairs to see what she wanted; she smiled at me and pointed down. I looked to where she was pointing and let out a shriek. There stood my brother Willie looking very handsome in his spiffy air force uniform. I flew down those stairs to hug him and hold on to him until he told me to go back upstairs and get some clothes together. He had stopped by for me to ride home with him. I didn't even think twice about not having put in a request for leave from work. I just asked Mrs. Moseley if she would call in sick for me the next day. It didn't take me long to be ready, and we were on our way. He'd gone from his base in Texas to New York where he lived and worked before enlisting in the military. He had borrowed a friend's car and now was on his way home to surprise our family. He had surely managed to surprise me.

I couldn't believe it, only a couple of hours ago, I'd been busy at my desk. Now here I was sailing along the highway on my way home to North Carolina with one of my special brothers. After we had cleared the maze of streets and roads in Arlington and reached the main highway that was South 301, Willie told me to settle down and go to sleep. He had two friends in the back of the car who were also going to visit their relatives in North Carolina. I managed to get comfortable, but sleep wouldn't come. I watched the dark sleeping houses and the trees fly by. There were no electric or outdoor pole lights along the countryside during that time, only the late moonlight on rooftops. The highway passed through the middle of each little town and then we were on a bright street with no bypasses. I never slept a wink and was awake when we passed over the North Carolina state line early in the morning.

After dropping the other two boys off at their homes, we headed for Iron Mine. I could hardly wait to see the family's reaction when we drove up. After turning off the main road by Mrs.

My brother Willie Herring and George Heggins at Fort Sill, Oklahoma.

Annie's house, we were on the narrow road that led directly to our farm. We saw that there had been recent rain and that the road was muddy in places. When we got near the old house that had been Mama's childhood home, the car got stuck in the mud. Try as we might, Willie couldn't pull it out. We looked, and there came Papa and Frank. They had heard the car and recognized that it was stuck and were coming to help, even though they had no idea who was stuck. You can imagine their expressions when they saw that it was two of their own that were in need of help.

We got out of the car to hug them both. Poor Papa was so glad to see one of his soldier boys come home safely, he cried, and I helped him cry. Then they all ordered me back in the car out of the mud, while they went about getting it unstuck. It didn't take long, and soon we were all in the house laughing and hugging each other. We could only stay at home for about four days.

Of course, there was always the unease and worry about Bennie being where he was. Willie took Mama to the hospital in Wilmington to see our beloved "Sis Gertie," as we had found that she was very sick. However, when we went to visit with her, we saw that she still had her cheerful smile and seemed so glad to see us. She was Mama's niece and was sister to Ethel and Mae (Bootie). Her son Lionel had been my best playmate and fighting partner when we were growing up. The few days that we could spend at home whisked by in no time, and after a tearful good-bye, we were again on the road heading north. All went well until we got to Chester County, Virginia, and another car pulled up beside us. A grinning, young White soldier looked at us, then spurted ahead. Willie's foot went down, and our car passed the other car, then he, again, passed us. I squealed and said, "Willie quit that." He was too busy catching up again to pay attention to me. I didn't have to worry long about the speeding of the two cars because there was another car that was speeding behind us with lights flashing. It was the highway patrol. The patrolman carried both cars and both drivers into the station, and they had to pay a fine right then and there. I think he was a little easy on them because they were both soldiers. It did, however, put an end to the racing. Willie was just as happy anyway, because he said the fun he'd had was worth the fine he'd paid for it.

When we reached Mrs. Moseley's house, it was well after dark. Papa and Mama had given me food from our smokehouse to take back with me. I had been given a whole cured ham, some sweet potatoes, and even some of Mama's strawberry preserves and sweet pickles. After the food was unloaded and stored in Mrs. Moseley's pantry, Willie said he'd have to keep going as he wanted to reach Buffalo as early as possible. It was such a long way back to Texas. I couldn't bear for him to just drive off and leave me at the house, so I said I'd ride as far as Pennsylvania Avenue and catch a bus back. It seemed that the ride didn't last very long before he was asking me where I wanted to get out. When we reached Eleventh and Pennsylvania Avenue, where I always caught the Arlington bus, I told him and his friends good-bye and didn't cry until after he'd pulled away. I watched the car until it was lost in the traffic.

On the bus going back home, I kept my face toward the window. Of course, I saw a lot of people who were obviously happy, and I also saw that many of them were sad. It was a very uncertain time, especially for those who were in the service. You never knew when or where you'd see them again. Each member of my family has always been very dear to me. No one could take another's place. That night, when I lay down to sleep, it seemed almost as if I was still riding in the car. It was a long time before I finally fell asleep. The next morning, Mrs. Moseley was delighted when I told her she could share my ham and potatoes. She also loved Mama's pickles and wanted to know how she prepared them. I didn't know except that preparation time took fourteen days. Now that I was ready to return to work, I had to go over to Dr. Willacy's office to get a medical slip. He was amused and asked what my ailment had been. I told him that was for him to decide, as long as it wasn't anything bad. I still don't know what excuse he gave me, but it was accepted at work, and life once again settled back into a routine.

# 9

# A Visit from Mama

*Through much that is hidden, life guides us along.*
*We believe in the singer, because of the song.*

R. H. Grenville

SIGNS of spring had started to appear. The oak tree outside of my window showed small swelling buds, the grass was turning green, and I caught the flu. I woke up one morning feeling terrible and asked Mrs. Moseley to call in sick for me again. I found out that Mrs. Mosely and her family had a horror of catching the flu. She and Doretha stuck their heads in the door to ask how I was feeling and said that they hoped I would feel better, but they came no closer to me. My mail was slipped under the door. The next morning Sylvia showed up at my house and took charge of me the same as Mama or Eunice would have done. She helped me get washed and put on a fresh nightgown. She then went up to the village, returning with orange juice, chicken soup, aspirin, and Vicks. After she had fed me and given me medicine, it was time for her to leave for work. No one will ever know how grateful I was for that girl. She'd proven to be a real friend. She was a

New Yorker, and I had often been told that people from New York were cold and unfeeling. To this day I feel good just remembering her.

I noticed on the calendar that Easter would be in April this year. I wrote and asked Mama to come spend the weekend with me. She was delighted and said that she would, in fact, come spend a week with me. I began planning for her visit. I wanted to have a new Easter outfit waiting for her and also wanted to send Eunice a new outfit. She was now back home again. I thought of all the pretty clothes that Eunice had bought for me while I was in school. Now I could do something for her. I decided that I would go over to Washington and search the same stores where Rhoda and I had gone shopping the first Easter I was there. I found a navy suit I thought would look good on Mama with a white blouse. I then found a navy hat and purse, as well as white gloves. I couldn't pick out her shoes because she had small, narrow feet, and she would need to try the shoes on first. For my sister I bought a lavender suit and a white blouse. I also bought lavender for myself.

With this done, I settled back into my routine to wait for the great day to arrive. We had a late snow, and Sylvia came over one Sunday morning to walk to the cemetery with me and visit the Robert E. Lee Mansion. I decided to carry a box of chocolates with me that were left over from Valentine's. The sun made the snow sparkle and glisten. When I opened the box of candy, Sylvia selected a nice piece and popped it in her mouth and started to chew but spat it out and tried to clean her mouth with tissue.

"What's wrong? Was it a bad piece?" I asked her.

"No, it was a really good piece, but I'm Catholic and it's Lenten season." I discovered that Catholics couldn't eat sweets during that period.

"Sorry, I'm Baptist, and we eat anything." Even so, I quit eating the candy since she couldn't enjoy it too.

When we entered the Lee home, it was like going back in time. The bedrooms were furnished with high canopied beds with white counterpane spreads, white curtains, polished wood floors, and a stool beside the bed to step on when getting in bed. One room looked as though someone had just gotten out of bed. An open Bible lay on a round table with wire-framed glasses lying on top of the Bible. There was a comfortable-looking rocking chair beside the bed, and coals were glowing in the fireplace. There was a boy's bedroom with a trundle beneath the bed. I had never seen a trundle bed like that before. It could be pulled out and pushed back under the bed. The drawing room was grand, and so was the dining room. The kitchen was in the basement of the house. It had cobblestone floors and the largest fireplace I'd ever seen. There were round black iron pots on chains that hung over the coals. There were iron doors in the wall beside the fireplace that opened to reveal ovens for baking. There was an array of long-handled iron spoons and forks for tending the food and low stools for the cooks to sit on. This was the winter kitchen. In the back yard was another building with a similar kitchen.

There was also a bedroom with a low homemade bed, a thin mattress with a patchwork quilt, a rocking chair, and a baby crib. It is said that the Black women, who were referred to as "mammies," lived in that room and kept whatever baby the White women, who were referred to as "mistresses," might have until the baby was old enough to have a room in the big house. I also read that the Black women nursed the baby in addition to caring for it in other ways. The baby was taken to the big house when the parents wished to see the child and spend some time with their baby.

There was a large dark wine cellar behind the winter kitchen. I'd never seen so many bottles on the shelves lining the walls. There were wooden kegs on stands around the floor and outside; the smokehouse was across the yard opposite the kitchen. This kitchen was used during the summer months to keep from heating the main house. Old dried-up hams hung in the smokehouse. Farther down were the slave cabins that we both decided we didn't care to see. It was an interesting visit. From the front porch, there was a beautiful view of the Potomac River and of Washington beyond the river. It was a lovely and peaceful place. It wasn't hard for me to be carried back to that long ago time and imagine the people who had lived here. I could imagine them sitting on the porch in rocking chairs, enjoying the lovely view of the river, Washington, and the surrounding countryside. When we left, we again stopped by the Tomb of the Unknown Soldier to watch the guard pace, pause, turn, and pace again. I never tired of watching that ritual and sometimes wished the man buried there could see how much he was being honored. There was only one "unknown" at that time.

Work at the office went on as usual. I spent many of my lunch hours with L. B. and didn't go down for lunch as often as I once did. She was such a nice, down-to-earth person and was so easy to talk with. A man who worked in our building lived in the country, or at least he lived where he had room for a chicken coop. He started to bring cartons of large fresh eggs to work, both brown and white, and would sell them for fifty cents a dozen. We mobbed him whenever he appeared in our office, giving him orders for the number of boxes we wanted. The next day he'd come in loaded with eggs to fill the orders we had placed. We started the habit of boiling eggs and bringing them to work for snack breaks. L. B. would typically devil some of her eggs. They were absolutely delicious. What with the meat and other food rationings, those eggs were mighty good.

The war raged on, and we hustled to keep track of our boys. It was about this time that we first heard of Dorrie Miller. He was a navy man and one of our very own. There wasn't much printed about him in the paper, but word spread around about the heroic deed he did. When the enemies were flying over the ship Dorrie was on and were machine-gunning everything that they could, Dorrie understood that the Black boys were not suppose to fire the ship's antiaircraft guns. At one point he saw one of the White boys killed while trying to shoot down planes. Dorrie ran out, pushed the dead boy aside, and started firing the gun himself. It was said that he shot down a large number of planes before he, too, was killed. It was many years later before he was publicly recognized and honored for what he did that day. All of us were both proud and yet sad over his fate, even though none of us knew him personally.

Once again spring was returning to Virginia. The grass was turning green, and the oak tree outside my window was beginning to show signs of budding. When passing the Tidal Basin, I could see that the cherry trees were getting ready for another spectacular display of their beauty. The trees in the cemetery were also budding out in tiny new leaves. The whole place looked fresh and bright, tender green. This, along with the rows and rows of white headstones in Arlington Cemetery, was an impressive view. In spite of the fact that it was a graveyard, it still looked pretty and cheerful. It seemed to be an appropriate place for our boys to be laid to rest. Although I enjoyed the beauty of the return of spring, I was always a little sad when winter passed. I've always loved the winter months, with the coziness of a warm fire at night and the sun shining on bright frosty mornings.

It was now nearing time for my mom to come spend Easter with me. I don't know who was more excited about her visit, Mrs. Moseley or me. Mama let me know that she would arrive on the Havana Special, which was a fast train traveling between Florida and New York. It only stopped in certain towns. Warsaw was the nearest stop to Wallace, so Mama was to take the afternoon train from Warsaw and would arrive in D.C. about one o'clock in the morning. Perfect, I thought, as that would give me time to get over to Union Station after getting off from work and meet her train. It was Good Friday, and Mama's new Easter outfit hung in my closet beside my own outfit, all ready for her.

The girls at work knew I was expecting Mama to arrive for a visit. Seeing how happy I was, they kept stopping by my desk to make some comment or would just smile when they passed. One of the new girls, Frances, said she would go to the station and wait with me if I wanted her to. I said that I would be glad for the company. She and I found seats right in front of the door where Mama was suppose to enter. There was a large clock nearby and a place that announced the arrival and departure of every train. It was now nearing the time that Mama's train was due to arrive. We chatted, bought snacks, and watched the crowds, always with an eye on the clock and the door. Finally it was time for the arrival and I stood ready to run the minute I saw my mom. People with baggage started to come through the gate. I looked at everyone as they passed me. Not one person even resembled Mama.

"She didn't come," I told Frances.

"Oh well, maybe she's on a later train," Frances said. "Let's wait for the next one." We sat back down and chatted a little more. By now it was after 2:00 a.m., and both of us were getting sleepy, so we dozed for a while, but woke up every time a new bunch of people arrived. Still, my mom did not arrive. Finally, Frances said she would have to go. I told her that it was all right for her to leave and thanked her for staying as long as she had. I said that I would stay a while longer. I settled back to wait longer, but I was too worried to sleep. I knew Mama wasn't used to traveling alone, and what with it being wartime with thousands of people on the move as well as the fact that it was Easter weekend, I was concerned. There was an elderly White man nearby who kept looking my way, as though he wanted to talk with someone. I guess I looked harmless so he started talking. I told him I was deaf, so with gestures and speech, he asked if I was waiting for someone to arrive. He later said good-bye and wished me good luck.

By now it was almost dawn, and I decided that I would wait until daylight and then leave. I'd finally given up hope of seeing Mama come through those doors. My eyes felt like they were full of sand as I dragged out to the streetcar island in front of Union Station and boarded the streetcar for Pennsylvania Avenue. It was almost sunrise when I arrived home and put my key in the lock to let myself in. When I entered, there was Mrs. Moseley up and beaming, looking behind me for her first glimpse of Mama.

"She didn't come," I said miserably and dragged on upstairs. There I found that Mrs. Moseley had gone all-out preparing for Mama's visit. She'd put up new curtains, a new spread had been put on the bed, and new scatter rugs were on the floor. The bed was freshly made, and the covers had been turned back. I was too tired, worried, and sleepy to care. I took off my shoes and outer clothes, said a short prayer for God to please protect Mama wherever she was, and fell into bed already asleep. I don't know how long I'd been asleep when I felt someone patting my head and kissing my check. When I opened my eyes, there was my mama bending over me. At first I thought I was dreaming, then I jumped up screaming MAMA!

Now I was full of questions as to where she'd been and what had happened. She told me that she had taken the bus from Wallace to Warsaw, but when she got to Warsaw, the train hadn't come, so she decided to stay on the bus to finish her journey. The only problem was that when she had to change buses along the way, the bus was already full and there were no available seats. She had a suitcase with her and decided to sit on the suitcase. There were more people standing. Among them was a young White sailor who Mama said looked so tired and very young. She asked if he wanted to share her "seat," and he gladly accepted and sat down beside her. They proceeded to get acquainted, as to where they came from and where they were going. He had been home on leave and was now on his way to be assigned shipboard duty, but he didn't know where he would be going. He showed Mama pictures of his family. Then the lights were dimmed so passengers could sleep, and the young man did so, with his head resting on Mama's shoulder. That's the way they rode into Washington, but the bus driver never bothered them. After all, it was her suitcase and it was toward the back.

When she arrived in D.C., she had contacted Cousin Mary, and Lloyd had driven her over to where I lived. Sleep was forgotten, and I was quickly out of bed running to the closet to show her the new outfit that I had bought her for Easter. She was surprised and happy with it. Then she showed me her surprises. She had sewn me two pretty cotton summer dresses and had bought food for Easter dinner that included a whole chicken and vegetables. I tried to get her to lie down and sleep awhile, but we were both too excited for sleep. After we had bathed and put on fresh clothes, we went downstairs to fix breakfast. She was delighted with where I lived, the town, the people, and everything. Most of all, she was pleased with Mrs. Moseley. It was as if they had always known each other. She had to take Mrs. Moseley upstairs to show her the Easter outfit I had bought for her. Cousin Mary called to say that Lloyd would be over the next morning to take us to church with them.

I got the idea of getting Mama's hair professionally done. Mrs. Moseley called her hairdresser, who worked across the pike, to see if she could do it. The hairdresser gave Mama an appointment. Later that afternoon we walked over there. I'd never been to that house before but had certainly noticed it. The house looked like a mansion. It was located back from the street, on a hill, and the beauty shop was in the basement. Mama's hair was trimmed, shampooed, pressed, and styled for the sum of three dollars. When we arrived back at the house, Mrs. Moseley told her how nice and pretty her hair looked. Mama said it was the first time that she had ever had her hair dressed in a shop. At home, most of the time, the neighbors did each other's hair.

Mama and I were up bright and early Easter morning, so we could have breakfast and be ready when Lloyd came to pick us up. When we were dressed, she allowed me to put a little makeup on her face to go with her new hairdo. When I was done, she looked very nice. Cousin Mary and Leroy were already in the car waiting for us. When we joined them, we went straight to the New Jersey Avenue Baptist Church, which the older members of the family attended. The younger members of the family belonged to the Salem Baptist Church, right across the street from their house.

I had only been to the New Jersey Avenue church once before, with Lloyd, Leroy, and Georgia. We chose to sit in the balcony. It was a huge church with balconies upstairs on each side. There were two choir lofts; one on each end with the main floor down below us. On this particular Sunday, it was Easter and some of the people in attendance must have been there since sunrise service. The sanctuary was packed. We had to wait in the vestibule until available seating could be found for us. Some empty seats were finally found toward the back of the church. We were grateful to have seats anywhere, and there were speakers so everyone could hear the service. Of course I could see and it was all beautiful, but I couldn't hear and churches didn't have interpreters in those days, but that was okay. I knew the Easter story and was happy just to watch Mama enjoy herself. Her hat had a nose length veil and sometimes when she cried she forgot to lift her veil and tried to wipe her eyes through the veil. Once Cousin Mary slipped her a piece of gum and she also got the gum tangled in the material of her veil.

After the service was over, she kept saying how much she had enjoyed it all and how beautiful the music and the singing had been. Cousin Mary was a little peeved because the ushers hadn't been able to find better seats in the sanctuary. Cousin Mary and her family wanted us to go home with them for dinner, but I told them that John C. was coming over from Aberdeen, Maryland, where he was stationed so he could see Mama and have dinner with us. I prepared the chicken and vegetables along with the other food I already had and it made a right tasty Easter dinner. While we were eating, the phone by the stairs rang and Mrs. Moseley told Mama the phone call was for her. Mama found this hard to believe because no one had ever called on a phone and asked to speak with her before. I followed her out into the hallway to see what the call was about. We were thinking it was probably someone from Cousin Mary's house. Wrong! It was her son Willie, calling from Texas to wish her a Happy Easter. I had told him that she was coming to visit with me. Now, this topped off everything.

After she came back to the table, Norwood stopped by to see Mama, and after dinner, we went over to Cousin Mary's. Both Norwood and John C. had dinner with us. The kids and I decided to ramble again, as it had been a while since we'd done that. When we got back to the house, the parents were all gone, but they soon returned home. Mama, still in a state of excitement, announced that she had been to see "Cousin Peter." I'd never heard of Cousin Peter, so she and Cousin Mary proceeded to educate me as to who Cousin Peter was and then told me about more cousins that I did not know I had. They had gone over to Baltimore to visit with these cousins. I escaped from the "cousin" stories and said to the kids, "Let's go to the store for ice cream," after which Lloyd drove us home. I didn't have to go to work the next morning, so Mama and I talked, caught up on home news, and discussed the different people she'd met and places she'd been. She loved it all. She also enjoyed watching the airplanes take off and land. Where I lived wasn't far from Andrews Air Force Base, and a lot of the planes flew low over the house and could be seen from my rear window. Each time Mama heard a plane overhead, she would run to the window to watch the plane for as long as it could be seen. At home Sam would tell Mama that when he got a job earning lots of money, he was going to build her a house with a glass roof over her bed so she could see all the planes fly over at night without having to get up.

The next day I couldn't wait to let the girls know that Mama had arrived after all, especially Frances, who'd been so kind to go and sit up there with me for such a long time. They all said that they were glad I hadn't been disappointed and hoped she would have a nice visit, and much to my pleasure, Mama was doing just that. After work, when I went upstairs that night, I was smiling at the thought of Mama being inside the house, asleep or maybe reading while waiting for me. She was doing neither. The room was just as empty as any other night. Now where was she? There were three chairs grouped in front of my rear window, so I guessed someone had been visiting her. I prepared for bed

and had a snack, and still no Mom. It was past 1:00 a.m. by this
time, and I was getting into a dither, wondering if she was sick
or had gone for a walk and gotten lost or what. I tried to just keep
calm and pray that she was all right, but I became more and more
nervous and scared. I looked at my watch and saw that it was past
2:00 a.m., close to 3:00 a.m. I opened the door to go down and
knock on Mrs. Moseley's door and see if she knew anything about
Mama's whereabouts. I didn't have to knock, because just as I got
to the head of the stairs, she opened the outside door and stepped
in. She was all happy and smiling.

"Mama," I shrieked, "where have you been?"

Still smiling brightly, she said, "Oh, I've been to a nightclub."
Like she'd been going to nightclubs all her life!

I was speechless, but managed to say, "You've been where?"

"To a nightclub," she repeated. She then told me that she had
not known she was going. Cousin Kinch had asked for the day off
work so he could cook Mama a meal like some of the meals he
cooked at the restaurant for the government bigwigs. And oh, had
he ever cooked her a wonderful dinner. She named a lot of different dishes that he had made for her, some of which I was not familiar with. After dinner they took her out to see the Capitol at
night, and then went to a club. She didn't know the name of the
club, only that Andy Kirk had been there with his band and they'd
played a song called "Swinging on a Star." I knew the song. I'd
never seen Andy Kirk, but now my mom had. He was quite popular at that time. I was still in a state of shock but told Mom to hold
off telling me about it until morning. I was weary of working most
of the night and worrying about her, so we went to bed. The next
day I got the full story of her night on the town. I was glad that
she had had the opportunity to enjoy herself and appreciated
Cousin Mary and her family for making it possible. I'd just never
thought my Mama would be going out to a nightclub, and I got

tickled when I thought of the times when I had come home late and she'd ask me where I'd been. Now, here I was asking her where she had been. Getting a dose of my own medicine, I'd say. I decided that in the future I would be more careful about the times I arrived home.

After this adventure, things became quiet again, and she would be home when I came in after work. I was trying to persuade her to stay for an additional week, but a phone call came for her to come home at once, because her brother Buddy Vatson was very sick. My mother's niece Ethel and Ethel's sister Mae (Bootie) were already there. I decided that I should go home too because I didn't want my uncle to leave us before I could see him again. We made plans to leave that same night on the Havana Special. Arriving in Warsaw next morning, we went straight to Buddy Vatson's house. I felt so bad seeing him lying there in bed so thin and looking very tired. Ethel and Bootie fixed a nice lunch of green beans, corn, and cold sliced ham. I didn't see them often enough, and it was good to see them again. All three of them had left home before I was old enough to recognize relatives. There were three of them who were sisters, and their mother was my late aunt Nancy. I never saw Aunt Nancy. Gertrude, the oldest, lived in Wilmington, North Carolina, with her husband, Benjamin, whom we called Mitchell, and their only child, Lionel, and often came to visit. Bootie and her husband, Bill, lived in Atlantic City, New Jersey. Ethel, the youngest of the three girls, had been living with Buddy Vatson and was a teacher in a nearby town. She later married and moved to New Jersey.

I remembered one occasion when they came for a visit with us. They were all so pretty. I used to wish I could be that pretty when I grew up. I was closer to Sis Gert since we saw a lot of her. She and Lionel would come and stay with us for a couple of weeks at a time. I always enjoyed those weeks. She was such a sweet person. She and Mama always had to untangle Lionel and me. Fighting seemed to be our favorite pastime, but we also had fun playing together.

On the day we were visiting Buddy Vat, he slept a lot, and all we could do was watch him in deep sleep. It was decided that Mama and I would go on home and return to his house when needed. We thought he was about to leave us then, but he rallied without showing any real improvement. Since I didn't have leave that would cover a long absence from work, I decided to go on back to my job. Eunice went back to Arlington with me. R. C. was still in D.C., so she stayed with Cousin Mary. However, I'd been back to work only a couple of weeks when Mr. Gaskins came to my desk with a message. A call had come to inform me that Buddy Vat had passed away. I had been anticipating this news, but it was sad just the same to think that I wouldn't see him anymore. I remembered how happy he had been when he came to my graduation. He met up with his old school friend who happened to be my principal. Mr. Gaskins and Mrs. Coates were very sympathetic and said that if I wanted to go to the funeral, it could be arranged. Since I had just traveled to North Carolina to see him while he was still alive, which is when it mattered the most, it seemed easier for me to just send flowers, which is what I did.

# 10

# Terrible News

*I trod the earth and knew it was my tomb,*
*And now I die, and now I am but made.*
*My glass is full, and now my glass is run,*
*And now I live, and now my life is done.*

Chidiock Tichborne,
"My Prime of Youth Is But a Frost of Cares"

LIFE was pretty much back to normal now. Spring was rapidly passing, and we were into early summer. The nights were warm, and we still didn't have central air conditioning on the fourth floor of the Annex, so we now had permission to go down to the ground floor and sit on the steps for our snack break. That was fun. Some of the girls would smoke a cigarette with their sodas. I enjoyed just sitting and looking at the Washington skyline across the river and at the Pentagon building with all those lights. Awesome! Life was peaceful again, if you could forget about the ongoing war for just a little while. However, for me this spring wasn't meant to be a peaceful one. There was yet another phone call and another sad message, this one informing me that Sis Gert had just passed away—Lionel's "mother dear," as he always called her. Sis Gert had been another person I loved dearly. I had missed my uncle's funeral, but I decided that I was not going to miss Sis Gert's also. Eunice and I took the next train home.

We left D.C. on a Saturday night, because the funeral was scheduled to be held on Sunday. We would return to Virginia on Sunday night. This way I would be back home by 4:00 p.m. Monday and would not need to request any time off from work. Our train would reach Warsaw in time for us to catch a bus for home, or so we thought. But, as the saying goes, "The best-laid plans of mice and men . . ." The bus that we had planned to catch had just pulled out for Wallace just as our train was pulling in. Another bus was due in an hour or so, but that would put us behind schedule. We fumed and fretted.

There was a guy at the train station with a big logging truck. He heard us talking and said that he was going to Wallace and that we could ride with him. We accepted his offer, although I had doubts about the wisdom of doing so. The truck was dirty and ratty–looking, and he didn't look much better himself. Also, his eyes didn't look just right to me. I wondered if he had been sipping moonshine. However, I wanted to make it to Sis Gert's funeral, so Eunice and I climbed into his gritty and raggedy seat, hoping that our clothes would stay clean enough in case we didn't make it to the house before the funeral began.

I didn't have long to wait before having my fears confirmed about the fact that the guy had indeed been sipping spirits. As soon as the truck pulled out on the highway, it started weaving from one side to the other. "Oh dear Lord," I prayed to myself, "Help us." He not only weaved, he started talking junk. I couldn't hear him, but I could tell by the way he looked. I sat by the door and told Eunice I was scared. I think she was scared also but didn't want to make him mad while he was driving. We were now quite a ways out of Warsaw, with only trees beside the road.

I kept quiet for a while, hoping that the man would get his head together and drive better. But when the truck gave a lurch toward the center of the road, I leaned forward to look at him. He wasn't even looking at the road. Instead he was looking at my sister, with his eyes all red and bleary. I glared at him, but he paid me no mind. He was too busy taking his hand off the wheel and putting it on Eunice's knee. I could stand it no longer. I had on a small hat with a long thin hat pin. Snatching the pin out of the hat, I jabbed the pin into the back of his hand and said, "Stop this truck and let us out of here right now." His mouth really started to work then. I couldn't hear it, so it didn't bother me at all. He did, however, pull over and stop the truck. I was out of the truck before it came to a full stop, with Eunice following right behind me. He lurched off still weaving. Eunice cussed "Oh highway patrol, where art thou?"

So, there we were in the middle of nowhere with no ride home. We saw another car coming toward us but were not sure whether to risk riding with another stranger. The car reached us, started to pass, then stopped quickly. It was our Cousin James, Uncle Foy's son. The Lord was with us! James looked at us, amazed to see his girl cousins standing beside the road on a sunny Sunday afternoon with suitcases. He told us to get in, and we lost no time in doing so. When Eunice told him what happened, he was very mad at the truck driver. He had just been to take a fare to Warsaw in his cab and was on his way back when he saw us. He took us straight home. When we went past the cemetery, I didn't see any cars ahead of us and was thinking to myself that the service at the church had not yet ended, so maybe we were, in fact, in time. As it turned out, there were no cars at the church because they had finished the service and had all gone. We saw that there was a new grave beside Buddy Vat piled high with fresh flowers. I said, "Oh Eunice, they've already buried her." Eunice nodded and we both cried.

When we got to the house, Papa was seated in a comfortable chair on the porch, surrounded by his dogs and enjoying the quiet afternoon. He and Mama were both surprised and glad to see us. They hadn't known we were coming and said they were sorry we had gone to all the trouble to get here. I didn't tell them about the truck driver for fear of upsetting them, and I don't believe Eunice told them either. The threatening incident was over, and I was just thankful that God had taken care of us, so why worry my mom and dad in the aftermath?

We enjoyed spending the rest of the day and the night with our folks and took an early bus back to Washington. Once again life settled back into its usual routine. Gregory and Corbin, the only two boys in our department, joined the service and left us. One of them joined the navy, but I was never sure which branch the other one joined. There was a void at work, as we missed them a lot. Howard requested, and was approved for, a few days off to go home to North Carolina to attend her eighty-four-year-old mother's wedding. This would be the fourth wedding for her mother. She was tickled to death and very proud of her mom. Howard had a son in his twenties and a young stepsister or half-sister who was near my age. I didn't see any of my deaf friends anymore.

While I was over in town shopping on Seventh Street one day, I ran into two of the boys with whom I had been friends at school. We stopped and chatted long enough to catch up on the news. It was a strange feeling to be able to stand close enough to the young men that we could touch each other and talk but not have to be afraid that there were teachers watching us so that we would be reprimanded. I told them I had seen some of the girls from school since I'd been living in the D.C. area. They had already heard that most of the deaf people lived near each other, with the exception of Thomasina, who lived in northeast D.C. I still often saw many of the people from Wallace, North Carolina. One day I was walking on Eleventh Street near Pennsylvania Avenue, when I noticed a man just ahead of me, walking in my direction. I moved aside so he could pass me, but instead of passing me, he again got in front of me. I looked at him, a bit annoyed, but then saw that it was a family friend from Wallace whom we called P. C. It was so good to see him, and we also stopped to talk.

One morning after I'd had breakfast and was preparing to mop the kitchen floor, the phone rang. Mrs. Moseley came to me frowning and with a piece of paper in her hand. She said someone had called and said for me to go to the address on the paper, but she didn't catch the name of the person who called. I looked at the paper but was not familiar with the address, which was in southeast Washington. In fact, I had never been in southeast Washington, as none of my friends lived there. Upon hearing me say this, Mrs. Moseley told me not to go since she could not give me the name of the person who called. Since I didn't know who it was or where I'd be going, I agreed with her and continued to mop the floor. As the day passed, I couldn't get the phone call out of my mind. Then I remembered that Mama had said that Ethel and Bootie had gone down to Florida to visit their dad and had told her they might stop in D.C. to see me on their way back north. I wondered if it could be them, or possibly one of the service boys with whom I had been corresponding. None of the boys had said anything about coming home, and besides, they would have come out to Arlington and looked me up. I finished with the floor, took a book out on the side porch and tried to read. Later I decided that I would ride over to see Cousin Mary for a little while. Mrs. Moseley had gone in her room.

I changed clothes, and headed for the bus stop. Upon reaching Pennsylvania Avenue, I decided to ramble about for a while before going to Cousin Mary's. A cab stopped right in front of me as I was crossing the street. I got into the cab and gave the cab driver the address that Mrs. Moseley had written down. I asked the driver to go by the house slowly so I could see if I recognized the place or anyone. When we reached the address, it was rows of neat yellow and white apartment buildings that sat a ways back from the street. I told the driver that I had never been here and wasn't sure who I'd see and asked if he would please wait until I checked. I told him that if I had not returned in ten minutes for him to send for the police or for someone to check on me. He agreed that he would wait. As it turned out, I didn't need help at all. When the door opened, there, stood my cousins Ethel and Bootie. One has never seen such joyful hugging and kissing. I felt someone hugging me around my knees. When I looked down, I was surprised to see a pretty little girl who was Ethel's only child, Jackie. I'd never seen her before. They were urging me on to another room to sit down.

I told them that the taxi was still outside waiting for me. Someone ran to the door and waved for the driver to leave. The driver did not leave, and then I remembered that he was waiting to be paid his fare. When I started outside to pay him, I was pushed back into the house. Bootie grabbed her purse and ran out to pay him for me. They were preparing breakfast and insisted that I stay and eat with them. I told them that I had already eaten breakfast, so they said it could be lunch. They introduced me to Lucille, the friend they were visiting with, and I later met her husband. They were very nice people. After eating, we sat around the table trying to catch up on all the lost time in the past years when we hadn't seen much of each other. Both Ethel and Bootie were just as sweet and kind as their sister, Sis Gertie, had been. Time flew by so quickly. I saw that it was time for me to leave in order to get to work on time, and someone called a cab for me. I had enjoyed visiting with them and hated for the visit to end. When the cab did arrive, I was hugged and kissed and bundled into the backseat. As the taxi started to drive off, they ran along beside the car waving and blowing kisses. What an absolutely wonderful time I'd had.

During the ride home after work, I thought of Mrs. Moseley and what she would say when I told her about my visit. She was in the kitchen when I walked in. After staring at me for a while, she said, "You went." It was a statement, not a question.

"Yes ma'am," I replied. She made a face, and I laughed. "It really was my cousins who called."

"But you didn't know that when you left here." I told her about the cab driver, and she also took a dim view of that situation.

"You didn't know him either," she said.

"No ma'am," I told her, "but in those times when I don't know what to do about a situation, I always ask God to guide me to do the right thing." She nodded and said that she was glad I had enjoyed my visit with my relatives but was also happy that I returned home safely. Then, shaking her head, she said that I amazed her. I really appreciated the concern from Mrs. Moseley and her family regarding my safety and well-being. I felt that God had blessed me when he guided me to her door.

The fresh and tender green of springtime was beginning to turn into the lush darker green of summer. I could smell the fresh dirt from Mrs. Moseley's newly plowed garden that was across the street. The smell of honeysuckle was heavy in the air, and it made me lonesome for home.

Since my sister was back in D.C., I took to going over to see her several times a week. Her husband was on another construction job in Front Royal. Also, her foot had been bothering her from time to time. The spring weather was so beautiful that I started to walk up Eleventh Street from Pennsylvania Avenue. It was the same as when I had lived over in that area. One Sunday morning I was trying to think of something to do. That problem was solved when my sister came over to visit me. Together, we went over to Miss Emmy's to see the other girls. Most of them had gone out for the afternoon, but Maggie was home. I proposed that we go for a walk.

"Where?" they asked me.

"Let's go for a walk in the cemetery." Eunice didn't think much of my choice, since she seemed to have a thing about cemeteries. However, Maggie was game and said she'd never been in the cemetery before. Having visited the cemetery previously, I showed them which gate to enter through.

Thinking back to past experiences, I said, "We better be out before six o'clock." It was so beautiful and peaceful there. I rambled about, reading inscriptions on headstones while Eunice and Maggie followed talking. Seeing a freshly dug grave, I decided to peep inside. I don't know exactly what I expected to see, but it sure wasn't the shovel full of dirt that was thrown upward and almost hit me in my face. I ran shrieking back to Eunice and Maggie to tell them what had happened. Not one to become easily excited, Maggie walked over to the grave, looked down, and said, "Hey, hant." A man's head appeared. He explained to Maggie that he'd stopped for a short cigarette break and hadn't heard us come up. I learned an important lesson that day, which was "never to be curious about open graves."

We completed our afternoon outing and were outside the gate well before six o'clock. I wished that I could carry them inside the Annex and show them where I worked, but we were absolutely forbidden to allow unauthorized personnel into the office area. We still had a nice day, and I think Eunice enjoyed the day as much as I did.

On another Sunday morning not long after the visit to the cemetery, I found myself facing another beautiful day with nothing to do. Having eaten breakfast, I sat in the swing and read for a while and then decided to wash my hair. I decided that the day was much too pretty to just sit there and waste the time. I decided to ride over to D.C. and visit with my sister since her foot was hurting her again. I decided to walk up Eleventh Street, since it was such a pretty morning, and do some window shopping. I stopped at a fruit stand and bought some pretty bananas and some other fruit to carry to Eunice.

I was tripping along, feeling very much at peace, when I noticed a taxi cruising along the street right beside me. The driver asked me if I wanted to ride in the cab. I shook my head, indicating that I preferred to walk, and continued walking. He continued his slow pace beside me until other cars forced him to speed up. He drove to the next intersection, made a right turn around the block, and came up beside me again. I decided that I would just ignore him. However, he drove ahead of me, found a parking space, and waited until I was close to him. He then opened the rear passenger door and motioned for me to get in. I refused and continued walking, but had grown very uneasy. There weren't many people around since this was a business district and it was Sunday morning. The driver was a middle-aged White man and had a rough-looking appearance. When I reached N Street, and he saw that I was going to cross there, he again went ahead of me and parked just before the intersection where I planned to cross to Tenth Street. Again, he opened the door and told me to get in, but I walked on at an even faster pace. When I stepped off the curb and started across Tenth Street, he started his cab up without even closing the door and came roaring around the corner trying to run me down. I guess my guardian angel helped me leap as fast as I did to get to the opposite side of the street. I could feel the wind and the heat of the engine as the cab went past me. I ran the rest of the way to Cousin Mary's house.

They were all angry and upset when I told them what had happened. The boys went out to see if they could find the cab and driver but they never did. When I did manage to calm my nerves, I had a nice Sunday with the family. When I was ready to leave, Leroy saw that I arrived safely home. I did not tell Mrs. Moseley about this incident, because I knew that she would be afraid for me each time I left the house. However, for a while after this happened I made sure that I rode the streetcar up Eleventh street. I never did see that man again.

At the office, one of the girls, Loree, had just given birth to her second baby, a little boy. Her husband was overseas in the war zone. She named the baby for her husband but said that the baby actually favored all the family—a nose like uncle somebody, eyes like somebody else. I asked her if her baby favored her in any way. Her answer was that he, in fact, looked like her "between the eyes." We all had a good laugh at this answer. I spent more lunch hours with L. B. because she was so easy to talk to—the same as talking with Mama. A new girl, from Georgia I think, had become very ill and was in the hospital. She was a pretty girl and loved to buy expensive hats with lots of frills. She would shop on her way to work and would bring her new hats into the office for us to look at. Now she was very sick and needed money for her hospitalization. We took up a collection for her. Another new girl had just joined us, and she was nearer my age. She also took a liking to L. B., so I, too, became friends with her. She was from New Orleans and always said she was Creole. The three of us shared a lot of time talking and sharing food.

By now it was July 1944, and the war still going strong. One day I received a letter from Maleon saying that he would be home real soon, which would be his last leave prior to being sent over to fight the war. That was both good and bad news. I was so happy that I would get to see him but, at the same time, was scared and worried at the prospect of his going where he would actually be fighting. I wondered whether there could possibly be a hiding place in the tail of a plane. He told me that he would be coming to Arlington and that I should be prepared to go on home with him for a visit. I still had a few days of annual leave that I had not used, so I requested a few days off. He didn't know exactly what day or time he would get to Arlington since traveling was so uncertain during this time. As it happened, he arrived while I was at work.

When I got home that evening, Mrs. Moseley said, "Your young man has been here."

"Maleon?" I shrieked.

"Yes, that was the name he gave, and he was tall and nice-looking." She also said that he had a friend with him and had to get back to his train. He wanted me to come on the next train and said that he would be waiting for me in Warsaw, which was his hometown.

I flew about getting ready, feeling like I was on cloud nine. The next day I caught the train to Warsaw. When we arrived and I got off the train, Maleon was the first person I saw. He was tall and handsome and was leaning against the car, watching for me. My legs seemed to get all mixed up, and I hardly knew which way I was going until he came to meet me. For the first time I wasn't embarrassed to be hugged and kissed in public, because I was so very happy. He took me to his home, where we spent most of the day while his mom cooked dinner for us. Showers of rain fell continuously, but the weather didn't dampen anyone's happiness. His mom was a tall woman. Her complexion was very light, and she wore gold-framed glasses. She had white hair that she wore in a knot. Her name was Mary, the same as mine. Toward evening, he took me on to my home. My mama fixed supper for us, and my brother Frank took him for a ride around the neighborhood. Papa and the rest of the family came in to shake his hand and acted as if they were glad to see both of us.

Later the two of us went for a long walk. I showed him my favorite places. By the time we started back home, the atmosphere was like our song, "In the Blue of the Evening." There was even a moon out that night, and everything was so beautiful. We were both so happy just to be together again. However, we kept things straight and proper and agreed that we both wanted to wait for marriage. Back during those times, people did, in fact, wait for marriage; at least most of them did, even during wartime. Neither of us had much time at home. He had about ten days and had spent half of it traveling from Oklahoma. I only had four days of vacation. The time flew by, and I had to be the first to leave in order to get back to work. Maleon was going to Greensboro to visit his college friends for a day or two, and then he planned to leave in sufficient time to stop over in D.C. again. It was agreed that he would call my house when he got there, and I would go over to Union Station if he didn't have enough time to get out to Arlington. It would be on a Sunday when he came through, which meant that I would not be at work. I stayed around the house all that day, but to my knowledge, no call came from him. I was terribly disappointed at not being able to see him one more time, but not upset. I had seen servicemen lined up, waiting with duffel bags to get on a train or bus, so I knew how hectic things could be. A week passed without my receiving any word from him, but I still did not find that unusual. The happiness from the previous week still filled my heart.

One night I dreamed that I saw him in an army transport truck. He was in the cab smiling at me and waiting for me to get to him, but there was a big puddle of wet clay and water between the truck and me. I couldn't cross the puddle, so I stood there looking at him and crying. I woke up and was actually crying real tears. After this dream, I couldn't get back to sleep, so I lay there just looking in the dark. I could see a chair across the room with the clothes I'd pulled off on the back of it because they were light or white. I finally managed to sleep a little more, but when I woke up, I kept thinking about that dream, and it bothered me. Later, when I started to look for clothes to wear to work, I noticed that the dress I'd worn the day before, the one I had left on the chair, was navy blue. None of the clothes on the chair were light colors. That puzzled me greatly, and I looked around for something white or light-colored that I would have been able to see in the darkness. There was absolutely nothing.

I dropped the thought and went on into the bathroom to shower and get ready for work. I had almost finished my shower and had started to get dressed when I heard a loud knocking. Thinking that it was someone needing the bathroom in a hurry, I called out, "OK, I'm coming on out."

When I opened the door and started out, Mrs. Moseley was just coming upstairs with a yellow paper in her hand that she handed to me. "This just came for you," she said.

I asked her if she had knocked on the bathroom door, and she said no, the only knock was that of the Western Union boy at the front door with the telegram. I looked at the paper Mrs. Mosely had handed me and saw that it really was a telegram for me. I stared at it for a moment but didn't want to open it. Mrs. Moseley waited with me while I hesitated to open the telegram. She seemed to know that something was dreadfully wrong. I just stood there. Finally, Mrs. Mosely took the telegram out of my hand, opened it, and handed it to me to read. I looked down at the words on that paper, and they did not make any sense to me because those words said that Maleon was dead. His father, Dad Stanford, had sent the telegram, and it also said that I would be further advised at a later date. He just couldn't be dead, as we had just returned from our visit down home. I read the telegram again and again, trying to force myself to believe those awful words. I looked at Mrs. Moseley and saw that her eyes were filled with water. My eyes were still dry because to me, this information was just not real. I couldn't cry over something that could not possibly be real.

"You aren't going to work, are you?" Mrs. Moseley asked me.

"Yes ma'am, I'm going to work," I told her. She tried to get me to call and explain that I couldn't go to work that day. She felt that I should go lie down for a while. "No, I'm going to work," I told her. I wanted to argue that I had to do something to occupy my mind.

I left the house, walking as usual. I knew that it was a bright sunny day, but it seemed that the sun was dark and I was completely numb. As soon as I signed in at work, it was obvious to everyone that something was wrong with me. I could not force myself to talk about it with anyone, at least not until lunchtime, when L. B. managed to get me to talk. When the other employees found out what had happened, they were all so very sympathetic, even Mr. Gaskins. I couldn't bear to go back to my room, the room where I had previously been so happy. Mrs. Moseley had called over to D.C. and told Eunice what happened. Eunice had left word for me to come over to D.C. with her. Leroy was waiting for me when I got there. He, along with everyone else, tried to understand how I was feeling. Eunice was there for me, trying to encourage me to eat something. The next day I went to work again, which seemed to be the only thing that was holding me together. Another day passed, and again I went back to my room, which seemed to be a strange place to me now. Mrs. Moseley told me that she would unlock the door that connected my room with Doretha's, so that I wouldn't feel so alone. I thanked her for the offer but assured her that it wasn't necessary. I wasn't afraid, and Eunice wanted me to go back and stay with her for a while longer. Everyone was trying so hard to help me get over this and to be myself again.

On the third day, another telegram arrived from Dad Stanford. This telegram let me know that Maleon's funeral would be held on August 10, in Warsaw instead of in Arlington. He said that if I needed someone to meet me, he would be happy to do so. Eunice did not feel that I should travel alone, but she was not able to accompany me because she was still receiving medical treatment for her foot. Eunice suggested that I wire some flowers and later go spend a few days with his family after things were over and settled down again. I desperately wanted to go to his funeral and be there for him. This would be the last chance I would have to see him again.

While I was still talking with Eunice, she handed me an envelope. When I looked at it, I saw that it was from Maleon. My first thought was that all of this had been a terrible mistake and that he was, in fact, still alive. I tore open the letter and looked at the date. Maleon had written the letter immediately after he arrived back to explain why he hadn't called as planned. When they reached D.C. during their return trip, they had only a little while before they had to leave for their destination. All of the pay telephones were busy. He had sat down to wait for a phone to become available, but when it did, it was time for him to go. He was very tired from the long ride, so the letter was short, but nonetheless very sweet. He said that he would write a long letter later, after he had rested some.

I saw that the letter had been mailed on August 2, 1944, and he was killed the following day. Five of the enlisted men had been riding in a transport truck just like the one I had dreamed about. They were meeting another truck, a gas tanker, whose driver had apparently fallen asleep and was driving on the wrong side of the road. Their own driver moved to the other side to try to avoid a collision, when the other man suddenly awakened, saw that he was driving on the wrong side of the road, and pulled back to his correct side of the road just in time to hit the other transport vehicle in a head-on collision. All five of the boys were killed immediately. The driver lived long enough to tell what had happened and then he, too, died. The only person who survived this horrible accident was the one who had caused it. I looked at the handwriting that was so familiar to me and could just picture Maleon writing this letter to me. It was then that I allowed myself to cry and grieve my loss. I simply could not stop crying.

By the next day, I had to admit to myself that I couldn't make it home alone. I decided to send flowers and a telegram, letting his family know how very much I loved them and that I would be home very soon. From that point on, I began to do some serious thinking, without confiding in anyone. Until now, I had been really happy in my job, with the friends I'd made, and with the places I had lived. I thought back to the call informing me that my uncle had died, then the call about Sis Gertie's passing, and now Maleon. Who next? I wondered. I asked myself what I would do if something happened to my mom, to Papa or to any other member of my family.

I was now twenty years old and had not lived with my mom since I was ten years old. My only time spent with her had been for three months each summer. My brothers and sister, except for Sam, were all grown up and had gone on to build lives of their own. We would never again be part of the same household, living together as a single family unit. I simply did not want to be away from home receiving telegrams and phone calls telling me that a member of my family had died. I simply wanted to be at home with them. I realized that my presence at home would not prevent bad things from happening, but I felt that at least I would be there with them and not away in a distant city receiving the news by telegram. In other words, I wanted to go back home to stay, back to Iron Mine and to my roots. I decided that I had spent enough time away from home and from my people. If I should decide not to return to Washington, I would still be able to financially support myself. I had saved some money and had a nice stack of war bonds that I had been buying each payday. The bonds were kept in a safe deposit box in a branch bank in North Carolina. I had also proven to myself that I was capable of getting a job, doing excellent work, getting along well with hearing people, and being financially independent.

I remembered seeing a girl at home on the streets with a box of Band-aids. She had put about three Band-aids in an envelope and also had ballpoint pens with imprinted cards asking people to buy them from her at a cost of one dollar, because she was deaf. I did not like what she was doing. The deaf people that I knew were skilled workers, and it was not necessary for them to walk the streets, practically begging, like she was doing. When the girl stopped and asked me to buy something from her, I tried to communicate with her in sign language, but she left in a hurry. I was never sure whether she did this because I was Black and she was White or because perhaps she wasn't really deaf.

I admire the fact that many people can make their homes in far-off places and be perfectly happy, but I knew, without a doubt, that I was not one of them. I gave a lot of thought to the decision I was about to make, but I kept these things to myself. I went to work as usual and did my job. Admiral Breedlove and another officer came in one day for all gold star workers to pose with them to have a picture taken. After he had given us certificates and pins, I found myself standing up front right next to him. Any other time this would have been thrilling, but now it had very little significance. I never knew what ever happened to the photos that were taken, because shortly thereafter, I wrote a letter of resignation to Miss Coates and Mr. Gaskins. They both made every effort to talk me out of leaving my job.

When it became evident to them that I did not intend to change my mind, they sent me to see a department counselor. The counselor spoke with me and even sent me down the pike on my lunch hour to get a statement from Dr. Willacy to determine whether there was any medical reason I should quit my job. As always, Dr. Willacy came through for me (bless him). He sent a letter back to the counselor stating that I had recently suffered the loss of several relatives and was thus depressed. He felt that I should take some time away from work, even if only temporarily. The counselor said that she would discuss the situation with my bosses and let me know later of their decision. The end result was that they would grant me three months' paid leave. This would allow me to go home to North Carolina, and they would forward my checks and bonds to me. If, at the end of the three-month period, I still wanted to quit my job, they would send me severance pay and my retirement, and my resignation would be official. They all still hoped that I would return. They told me that I had been one of their best employees, and they didn't want to lose me. I was touched by their words and cried a little, because I had never thought that my being there had made a significant difference one way or the other.

After getting everything settled, I told my coworkers that I would be leaving. They said that they would miss me but felt strongly that I would be coming back. It was much more difficult for me to tell Mrs. Moseley and Cousin Mary that I had decided to leave. They both wanted me to stay. I told Cousin Mary how much I appreciated all that she had done for me. I also let Mrs. Moseley know how much I had enjoyed living in her home. I told her that if I didn't come back to stay, I would surely return to visit and would never forget her, and to this day, I have not forgotten her. After all the years that have passed, even as I write this book, I can still see her face and the house, especially my room and the cozy corner by the radiator where I spent so many hours reading and eating chocolates.

Eunice came over to help me pack. She had accepted my news without saying very much. She only said that she would go with me to help me since she was accustomed to going and coming herself. The day finally arrived when I had to say good-bye to the muster-roll section and check out for the last time. Lloyd drove the family car over to pick me up. After loading my trunk, bags, and boxes of books in the car, I went back to hug Mrs. Moseley and Doretha, who had stayed home from work that day. They both assured me that they had loved having me stay with them. They felt that I had been a good tenant and said that the room would be there for me if or when I should come back. When we drove off, they were both standing in front of the screen door crying, and I was in the car doing the same. We passed Miss Emmy's and I reminisced that that was where I spent my first night in Arlington and also that it was the first time I had stayed in a house that dated so far back in history. It had front and back stairs, odd little rooms, and nooks in the attic, a back porch, and old apple trees.

I had already said good-bye to Maggie and the other girls. Laura was also thinking about going back home. I had never thought that it was possible for me to feel this way about any place other than my home and my old school. During the time that I had been here, I had grown from a young girl fresh out of school into a responsible adult. I knew that this would always be a part of me. Would I come back? I didn't know yet, but the door was being left open for me to return should I want to. I only knew that I desperately wanted to see my mom, talk with her, and see how it felt to be home again. Cousin Mary decided to take her yearly vacation down home to visit with her sister Cousin Hattie and her brother, Olcie. The entire family was going, so I didn't have to say good-bye to them. She and the younger children rode in the car with her husband and Lloyd. The other members of the family rode with Eunice and me on the train.

As usual, it was a hassle trying to travel. We had to take a regular train instead of the Havana Special that we usually rode. This train looked old and sort of grimy, and it stopped in every little town it passed. I tried to concentrate on reading so I wouldn't dwell on how happy I had been when I took this same route just a few short weeks ago. I could always hear the long lonesome blast of the whistle when it blew, and I hated that sound. That was one of a very few things that I didn't want to ever hear. The trip was hot and tiresome, as there was no air conditioning. When we opened a window for some cool air, cinders and soot blew in. The others were laughing and having fun about any little thing in order to help pass the time. I continued to read and could not force myself to look at Warsaw when we passed through.

Eventually, we arrived home, and we were some very grimy and soot-covered people. I had been unable to get all of my books in my trunk and suitcase, so I had filled a shopping bag with books. Now, as we gathered up our things to disembark the train, one of the handles on the bag broke and the books spilled out. Everyone helped to gather them up. Eunice told me that next time I moved someplace, she hoped she wouldn't be anywhere near me. When we finally reached the house, I went straight to

Mama. Her arms were ready and waiting. The family had fun laughing at our dirty faces. Maxine was growing up very quickly, and Marion (or Nod as we called her) was a toddler. Lattice stood close by, and I knew that she was ready for the two of us to get together and talk again. My baby brother Sam, only he wasn't a baby any longer, was quite tall and was about to graduate from school. It felt good to be back home among my people and to see that all were doing well, Eunice stayed home a few days and then she returned to D.C. I missed her a lot. In the midst of a crisis, she remained calm and level-headed and could maintain a good sense of balance. She was not known to pitch hissy fits, like me. It felt good just being around her. She told me that at least I knew that Maleon had loved me when he died, and I had fond memories of him.

Mama liked to go to bed early on summer nights and would lie with her head by an open window, looking out at the darkness of night and the stars. I would often go lie beside her, and we would talk. In the beginning, I would cry, and she would just pat me or smooth my head, but now we had in-depth talks. I told her about my decision to quit my job and come home. I also told her that the bosses wanted me to return to work in three months. I asked her what she thought I should I do. She said that it was my choice but suggested that I let it rest for a while and make a decision toward the end of three months. So that is exactly what I did. Mother Stanford had expressed that she wanted me to spend some time with her, which would be like going to yet another home. There was no one at her house now except the boys, Pete and Lloyd, who were both teenagers. I believe Pete was now seventeen, and Lloyd a few years younger. Paris was still at Tuskegee with the airmen. Dad Stanford worked at the shipyard in Wilmington, North Carolina, leaving home before day and getting in after dark.

On the first night of my visit with the Stanford family, I had gone to bed and, surprisingly, fell into a deep, peaceful sleep. Something woke me up, and when I turned my head, Dad Stanford and Mother Stanford were both standing beside my bed. He was bent over and kissed my cheek, as if I were a two-year-old. It showed me that love goes on. I felt good and peaceful being there with the family. In the mornings, while Mother cooked breakfast, I went out back to feed the rabbits and chickens. Pete was employed, but I don't know where, and Lloyd spent most of his time rambling around. Mother sewed a lot, and I would sit near her reading. Sometimes we would walk up the street to the grocery store, and other times, we just talked, mostly about how she wanted the house remodeled and about her school. She taught school in the next town, which was Magnolia. I enjoyed being there with her, and she seemed to enjoy my company. She told me that she did not have many friends, as she was quiet and reserved and didn't easily make new friends. She filled her time with her work, teaching, sewing, and taking care of her menfolk. She had no other relatives who lived in Warsaw, as she came from another county. I suspected that she was sort of lonely. A strong bond of affection grew between us. She said that she had always wanted a daughter and asked me to call her Mother, and so I did. It felt a bit awkward at first because I had never addressed any other woman as a mother, besides my own dear mom. However, since I called her Mama, or Ma, I wouldn't be using the same name. When I asked her about the question of whether or not I should return to work, like Mama, she felt that I should wait and make my decision at a later date. She also said that if I chose to stay at home, she wanted me to stay with her half of the time. I laughed and said that they would soon tire of having me underfoot.

I was still at their house the day the big box arrived with Maleon's personal belongings. We carried the box into the boys'

Maleon's funeral on August 10, 1944 in Warsaw, North Carolina.

bedroom and opened it. Everything was packed neatly and smelled of his shaving lotion, and cigarette smoke, as if he had just taken them off. My letters to him were tied together in a bundle. Also included in the box were pictures and the leather shaving case that I had sent him for Christmas. We remained quiet while we unpacked his belongings. Each of us had our own thoughts and memories of Maleon. She told me that I could take anything I wanted. I decided to keep a garrison cap but left the other items to be placed in a case his mother was having built for them. She had also saved me a bouquet of flowers from his funeral. I put the flowers in a vase and placed it on top of the piano next to his picture. She had also taken pictures of his funeral, which I still have. Mother Stanford told me that they wanted to take me to visit his grave whenever I felt that I was ready to go. Mother Stanford, Pete, Lloyd, and I visited the cemetery one Sunday evening. The cemetery was next to a small wooded area a distance from the highway. His grave was covered with cement with his name inscribed on it. This was the first time I had ever seen a vault. His family described to me the way it looked inside, and I felt that he was safe and secure. After this I began to feel at peace and more like my old self again. Maleon was at home, near the family who loved him, and not out in the open, fighting a war in some strange country. The war could never again hurt him. He had lived only twenty-four short years, but he had lived a good clean life and would continue to live on in the hearts and memories of those who had loved him.

Now I knew exactly what I was going to do. I, too, had returned to my roots and was back among those who were precious and dear to me. It was here in this place that I would live for as long as God willed me to live. No matter what happened, I would be with my loved ones and not in a faraway place reading a telegram or getting a phone call informing me that a loved one had passed.

# 11

## Big Decision

*Happy the man whose wish and care*
*A few paternal acres bound*
*Content to breathe his native air*
*In his own ground.*

Alexander Pope,
"Ode on Solitude"

I STILL had moments when I wasn't sure whether I was going to stay home or return to Washington. I'd go out to the pond, read my letters, and think about Arlington and the Navy Annex and my friends. Sam was in his last year of high school and driving the school bus. He'd come in, do whatever chores he had to do, then tell me, let's go out on the highway. Norman Hayes, my cousin who'd also gone to school in Raleigh, in the Blind Department, was out by then and had reopened his grandmother's country store. He sold the usual—groceries, sodas, candy, etc. He also had a jukebox, so, of course all the kids hung out there. They'd named the store Do-Drop Inn.

Quite a few of the old crowd had moved away or were still in service. Gladys, Berthena, Lou Evelyn, and Ella Louise had all moved to Philadelphia. James Arthur and Ellery were navy boys. Willie was still in the service. Thelma's brothers had all moved away. Harding was still in the service and married to a Florida girl. There were still lots of young people though—Thelma, Doris, Dot Bennett, Otelia, and her sister Fontaine, and Gladys's sisters, Ruth Mae and Beck, and their brother Elmo. They all went out of their way to welcome me back home. I gradually started feeling more like my old self again. They were all so lively and funny you couldn't be sad around them. Then there were cousin Mary Frank's girls, Caroline (Cat), Pearlene, and youngest daughter Geneva, or (Gen).

It was good to be home. By now it was early fall, or Indian summer—my favorite time of the year. I still spent a week with Mother Stanford, or mostly weekends, since she was back in the classroom teaching. Sometimes she'd come to see me and bring with her my old teacher Mrs. Beatty, who was teaching in Warsaw. Then Maleon's brother Paris was in a plane crash while in training. He survived, thank the Lord. After getting out of the hospital and going through rehab, he received a medical discharge and came home. One day he came with a small box and told me to open it. When I did, I found a beautiful birthstone ring. He and his mom had been to Wilmington and bought it for me in place of the engagement ring Maleon was to give me. It was wonderful how good and loving people could be. I felt humble and very grateful for so much kindness.

Being as it was fall, there wasn't much work to be done on the farm. Harvesttime was over. Tobacco had been graded and sold. I spent time with Lattice and her two little girls. I followed Mama around and talked. I also roamed the fields and woods with my dogs. Sometimes it seemed I'd never been away from home, that the time I'd spent in Washington and the Navy Annex, and all I'd been through had been a dream. However, it was far from a dream. A letter came from the Annex inquiring as to what I had decided to do. Time was about up. I had to face reality. I compared my life as it had been three short months ago to what it was now. I thought about Cousin Mary and her family, the fun I'd had with Leroy and Elnora, the Navy Annex, and all my friends, my room at Mrs. Moseley's, and the family. I thought about the time spent reading Maleon's letters and dreaming of the future, and how all of that ended that hot August day. Here in Iron Mine, I was home with my family. I'd been away for the better part of almost ten years. I knew I would not be happy in Arlington or Washington ever again.

I wrote my letter of resignation, thanking all of them for all their kindness and patience. I felt sad but, at the same time, relieved. I had made my decision, and it was over. I received another paycheck and then my severance check and the last of my bonds that I'd bought. I think Mama was sad too. She'd been so proud of me having that job and the life I'd lived up there, but I know she loved me and was glad to have me home with her. As usual, Papa felt I was exactly where I should be. And Sam, oh, the fun we had. Sometimes we went to the store the long way, around by the road, and we would stop in at Cousin Bert's house, where Doris would join us and sometimes Thelma. But mostly we took a path through the woods that came out behind the store. There we'd all have fun, sharing Cokes, candy, whatever we had, and playing the jukebox. They had a favorite record to dance to, "The Honey-drippers." It was played so much I got so I could recognize the beat when it came on. Kids from other neighborhoods started coming over. We made friends with them. One group was the Williams sisters, Dorothy, Mary, and Thelma, and their brother Joe Jr. Another was the Murphy boys, Frank, Willie, J. Johnny Lee, and C. H., as well as kids from Newton's Cross Road, Harrells, and other places. I found so many new friends, young and old.

Frank bought Sam and me a small green car called a Willys. It had seen its best days, but Frank patched it up and it would go, at least for a while. The time we had with it! We'd fill it with as many people as we could get in it, and away we'd go. We were just as proud as if it were a luxury car. It's a good thing we had lots of people in there. The time came when we needed their manpower. One Sunday we decided to give Leroy, who'd come from the marine base in Jacksonville, North Carolina, for a weekend visit, a ride. We went in town for a movie. When we came out, our transportation had decided it didn't want to take us back home. No amount of tinkering and coaxing would start it up. The boys had to get behind and push while Sam steered and we girls shrieked. We sailed through front street full-speed propelled by boy power. It finally cranked up and came to life, backfiring like a pistol. We didn't cut the motor off on the way home. We just paused long enough for each passenger to jump out at their home.

One day I suddenly realized Sam and his friends were giving me back something I'd missed—the normal teenage fun I couldn't have because of the school rules in Raleigh, where we couldn't even speak to a boy or young man unless told to do so under watchful eyes. Kids were expelled from school for good just for being caught signing to each other from a distance. Now, I was out of my teens, but it didn't matter. The Iron Mine kids were giving me back a piece of my life. I loved them all. There was another girl I became good friends with, Lettie McEachin. I'd known her as a baby, but then didn't see her around. She was at Sunday school one Sunday, and I was surprised to see she'd grown into a tall attractive young lady. There was a quiet dignity about her that I liked. I found she was an expert at fingerspelling, since she had a deaf cousin, Robert. He was still in school where I'd gone. I also found she loved to read the same types of books as I did. It wasn't long before we were fast friends, swapping books, discussing them and many other things. I really enjoyed being with her.

# 12

# Back Home

*The trees are in their Autumn beauty*
*The woodland paths are dry*
*Under the October twilight the water*
*Mirrors a still sky.*

W. B. Yeats,
"The Wild Swans at Coole"

LIFE was good again. All of us attended Sunday school every Sunday. My cousin Capjack was the superintendent and asked me if I'd teach the Beginners Class. Now that was a real honor, when at one time I couldn't even have a part in a program. He told me he knew I could do it. I didn't disappoint him, and I enjoyed teaching the babies. They couldn't read yet, so I'd explain the picture on back of their cards then read the story to them and ask questions. I didn't have any problems communicating with them. Last, I'd have one of them take up the collection. They all had nickels, dimes, or pennies, and this was carried up front to the collection table. Once our lesson was concluded, we quietly took seats up near the front of the church, where everyone gathered for the closing by the superintendent. Outside, we'd gather to walk home. Most of the time some of the girls would go home with each other for dinner, then we'd all spend the rest of the evening at Do-Drop Inn. By now we had two more stores we could visit. North of us was Jot 'em Down, and just down toward the creek was old man Walter Johnson's store. All of the stores sold the same kinds of things.

I was out of touch with most of my old school crowd but received mail regularly from Washington and Arlington. Cousin Mary had enrolled in a school to train to be a licensed practical nurse (LPN). All of her children were in school by now. Leroy and Lloyd had finished, and Leroy had joined the marines at Camp Lejeune. Lloyd had a government job at the Treasury Department. Georgia was a steno at one of the downtown buildings. Mrs. Moseley and Doretha kept me up-to-date on Arlington Village at the Annex. Sylvia was about to be transferred back to her hometown, New York City, as was Choisy. Sophie had been promoted and had her own office. I found out I'd been in line for a promotion as well. Reading all this, I felt a little nostalgia, but I never regretted my decision to return to Iron Mine. The times I liked best were when I was sitting on the end of the porch with Mama late in the afternoon or early dusk and just talking. It was so peaceful and serene, and I was so thankful to be where I could see, touch, and hug my mom whenever I had a notion to.

The war was still being fought, and Bennie was in the midst of it somewhere in France or Germany. Willie had transferred to the infantry and was in Arizona looking to be shipped to the Pacific someplace. That was our main worry. Paris was at home in Warsaw by now, waiting for his arm to heal. It was still in a cast. He'd come spend a few days with us and follow Papa in the woods when he went hunting. He couldn't use his arm to shoot, but he enjoyed the walk and watching Papa, who was an expert at all types of hunting and had good marksmanship.

One Sunday afternoon I was out walking with a bunch of the girls when Sam drove up in Papa's truck with his fishing boat on

the back and loaded with watermelons and some of the neighborhood boys. We were told to hop in, that he was driving us to
Black River over in Sampson County. This was a surprise to me,
since we didn't usually have such privileges with Papa's truck and
boat, especially the boat. When I started making inquiries, he
ignored them and told me to get in. Upon reaching Black River
Bridge, the guys unloaded the boat while we girls selected a
couple of nice watermelons and found a shady and sandy spot by
the water and started enjoying them. They were so good, cool and
sweet and juicy. A few of the boys got in the boat and went for a
short ride, but mostly they preferred to gather on the opposite
side from us, roll up their pants legs and wade in the shallow
areas.

One of the McEachin boys, Edgar, decided he wanted to take
a swim. Going a little farther down, he stripped to his shorts and
went in the water. At first he seemed okay, then he found he was
in really deep water. We couldn't see him from where we were
munching on watermelon and didn't know anything was amiss
until one of the boys, James "Scott" Wright, a newcomer, left off
cutting another watermelon for us and started running for the
bridge. He crossed to the other side and ran toward the group of
boys gathered in a knot trying to reach limbs and sticks out into
the water. We just could see Edgar's head bobbing above the
water. James jumped in, reached him, got a good hold, and pulled
him out. This scared us so bad it put an end to our fun-filled afternoon. The watermelon lost its taste. The boys fussed over Edgar,
got him dressed and into the truck, and hooked up the boat. It
was a somber group of kids who rode back home. Edgar was so
grateful to James for saving his life he tried to give him all the
money he had, which was a dollar. The news spread over Iron
Mine before nighttime that one of the boys had almost drowned
and that it was Ben Herring's son and daughter who'd carried

them to the river. When Papa came in about dark, he'd already heard the news, and his face was like a thunderstorm. He wanted to know what the devil we young'uns meant, carrying his boat off like that? When he'd finished, he told us from now on to keep our hands off his truck and boat. Those orders lasted only until Sam asked for the truck again, but we never again bothered the boat.

# 13

# Together Again

*Nature is fine in love and where it is fine*
*It sends some precious instance of itself*
*After the thing it loves.*

Willam Shakespeare,
*Hamlet*

WINTER had set in, and Iron Mine was quiet. The teenagers
were busy with schoolwork. Many of the adults had found jobs
working on base at Camp Lejeune and Camp Davis. Jacksonville,
North Carolina, had overnight become a boom town. The men
and women who worked there were making more money than
they ever had before. They built a dormitory on base for workers, and some rode back and forth daily on buses, cars, or trucks.
Eunice had moved back home as well and found a job she liked
at Camp Lejeune. After she helped me move back to Iron Mine,
she first returned to D.C. but things weren't the same. She and
R. C. divorced and she came back to North Carolina. She chose
to live in the dormitory and be close to her job so she wouldn't
have to ride so far every day. She came home for weekends.

Other Iron Mine women also worked there, including Cousin
Mary Liza, her daughter Nancy (Coochie), Fanny Bell, Annie
Ruth, Bertha, and her sister Edna. The last two were newcomers

from Sampson County. They lived at the end of the Bay Road,
south of our house. Bertha had married Walter, the oldest son of
our neighbors, Mr. Eva Murphy and his wife, Miss Lou. Bertha
and Walter had five children, who became friends with Frank and
Lattice's little girls, Maxine and Marion (Nod). I got to know and
enjoy all of them—Jean and Evelyn, the two oldest; Charles, the
one little boy; Patricia (Tricia); and Geraldine (Gerl), the baby.
All were pretty children. Jean had short curly hair like I had when
I was a child. She was quiet and tried to look after the rest of them
when they came to play. Evelyn was a sturdy little girl with long
thick black braids. I didn't see her smile much, but she sure
talked. One day I saw her and some of the other kids in the back
of Papa's truck. They were all dancing to some music coming
from somewhere, and Evelyn was saying shake it up and go. It
tickled everybody. Charles, their little brother, sometimes didn't
seem to know what to do with so much female company and
would just stand watching them. Tricia, too, was quiet. Her hair
was the longest and very red. Gerl, the baby, was the same age
as Nod, so they formed a baby friendship. She was round and
chubby with red cheeks and thick brown braids. Their grandmother, Mrs. Sally, stayed with them while their mother worked.

These children attended the same school I did as a child. Iron
Mine Elementary still had two rooms, a wood heater, and water
in a bucket from a nearby well. I enjoyed watching the children
play. Nod and Gerl were busy, outgoing little girls, forever getting into mischief, while Jean tried to keep them in line. Evelyn
and Maxine found other things to do. Tricia lived with her Aunt
Edna in another town and was only home for visits. I found her
a lovable child. She'd stay close by me not saying anything, but
it seemed I always understood her perfectly. I enjoyed having her
around. Nod and Gerl were the babies, and it was fun watching
them try to learn to play and keep up. Maxine had discovered the

joys of fairy tales. She called them Timey Tales, and each night I had to tell her a couple before bedtime. And so slowly, my life was again becoming peaceful and pleasant.

Once again Christmas was coming on. In spite of having children to enjoy the thrills of Santa, toys, and good things to eat, for the rest of us it was quiet and somber. Our boys were still in Europe and the Pacific getting hurt or killed every day. It was so good to be home to help clean, bake, shop for gifts, and join in all the other activities that go in for a happy Christmas. Only the worry and concern for Bennie and Willie were still there. We'd already sent them boxes, cards, and letters, and yes, our prayers too. Papa absolutely refused to even acknowledge it was Christmas Day. He refused to change from his hunting clothes or sit down and eat breakfast with us or open his gifts. His dogs, mules, pigs, and outdoor activities seemed to be his only consolation. He would prowl from room to room, then go outside to sit surrounded by his dogs and puppies, then make a trip to the stables, the pig-pens, and back in the house again. This went on all day. I know Mama was just as concerned about her boys as he was, but her unwavering faith in God was seeing her through.

So the Christmas of 1944 passed, and life went on as before, more or less. April rolled around, and we were on our way to C. W. Dobbins High School to attend Sam's graduation when word came over the radio that our longtime president, Franklin Delano Roosevelt, had died of a stroke while at his vacation home in Georgia. The news came as a terrible shock. He was the only president I'd ever known, and I guess I took it for granted he'd go on being president. It put a damper on graduation. It was all the people gathered at the schoolhouse could talk about. Some cried, Mama and I among them. They recalled how he'd brought them out of the Depression by creating jobs, Civilian Conservation Corps camps, and other things. I have always thought it would have been great if he could have lived a few more weeks to rejoice in the happy outcome resulting from his leadership and service to our country.

On May 8, 1945, the European War ended. There's no way I can describe the relief and happiness everybody felt. At first it seemed unreal, after four years of fear of bombs, worry about our loved ones, and rationing. Were we really going to have peace and plenty again? Not at once, as it turned out. The war in the Pacific still hadn't ended, and then we heard that some of the boys who'd been in Europe were being sent to the Pacific after a short stopover in the states. We heard from Bennie. He was whole and safe, thanks to the Lord, and hopefully would be home before too much longer. Willie was training in the infantry and would probably be sent to the Pacific, so we still had worry and fear with us.

Spring came again, and summer passed as before. There was hard work to do on the farm, and Sam was getting ready to enter North Carolina A&T University. The last of the green tobacco had been put in the barn, and the fall work wasn't due yet when the time arrived for Sam to take his departure. Since he was a freshman, he had to be on campus earlier than the other students. The early fall rains had started, and water was so high Papa and Frank had to leave the car and truck parked out on the highway with Sam's luggage already in it. On the day he was due to leave, Mama fried chicken and cooked other food for his lunch to take with him, as she'd done for me when I was leaving for Raleigh all those years ago. Since Eunice was working in Jacksonville, Mama, Lattice, her little girls, and I were the only ones there to see him off. After he'd bathed and dressed and packed a bag to carry by hand, he slung his shoes over his shoulder, put his lunchbox on one arm and his bag in the other hand, and with pants legs rolled to his knees, started on his journey away from home, after we'd hugged and kissed him as long as he'd let us.

Although he'd just turned eighteen, he looked so young. He looked about thirteen or fourteen. It just tore me up seeing my baby brother leaving home as I'd had to do at an even younger age. I could see it affected him too. He tried not to show it by frowning at me and telling the babies good-bye. He started off, wading through water a half-leg deep. Mama and I watched as far as we could see down the bay road. As he passed from sight around the curve, Mama broke down and cried too. Little Nod, ever the curious one, wanted to know, "Where Sam gone?" We told her he'd gone off to college.

The word *college* reminded her of a poem Mama had recited to her sometime before. It was:

You go to high school. I'll go to college
and come back here with a head full of knowledge.

Nod's version was: "You go to high school, I go college, come back here with my head all knotted up." Then she decided to sing, "Who 'Frew' the Whiskey in the Well," and "Pistol Packing Mama." When she reached the part of the song that said "Lay that pistol down, babe, lay that pistol down," she started dancing to her music. It was so funny. We were laughing and crying at the same time.

And so, my baby brother was off to college; whether he'd come back with his head all "knotted up" remained to be seen. His going left a huge gap in our family. He'd never been away for any length of time before, and we really missed his goings and comings, bringing neighborhood news and having his pals come by to see him. There were no phones that he could use at the college in order to let us know how he was doing, and we had no address to write him. Yet at the end of the first week, he showed up. He'd met someone from our area in Greensboro who was coming our way, and he'd gladly caught a ride and come home too. It was like he'd been gone for a year, we were so glad to see him, but we were sad again when he went back that Sunday. It wasn't as intense as the first time we said good-bye, and this time he left his address so we could write him. He made good use of the mail. We regularly got letters from him informing us that the food was bad and he was starving to death. Then he wrote us about some upperclassmen who were making him and some other freshmen make beds, wear skullcaps, etc. I realized he was being pledged to join a fraternity and knew these difficulties wouldn't last long. He wrote as often as he could find a stamp. He always needed change and wanted food from home. He'd found Cousin Helen Blackmore's daughter there, and her boyfriend Gillis, so he wasn't alone. He was in ROTC and sent a picture of himself in uniform. I guess he had come to terms with the fraternity, because he soon joined it. Then he needed new "threads" (clothes). The ones he had were "in tatters."

So, this set of kids was also growing up and leaving home. Doris and Ruth Mae had married. I still had Lettie and Dot Bennett. Edna had moved to Philadelphia to live with her dad. Most of the boys had been discharged from service and were back home. As soon as Bennie came back, he packed up Mable and the kids and came to spend a night in his boyhood home. It seemed the whole family went out of their minds with joy over being together again. And Bennie didn't have a scratch. Eunice, Lattice, and I cooked pots and pans of food while the children ran each other over the house, shrieking the whole while. Willie hadn't been discharged as yet, but it wasn't long before his assignment to Hawaii was over and he too came home from the war, and life was peaceful once more.

# 14

# Victory at Last

*Beauty is truth, truth beauty—that is all*
*Ye know on earth*
*And all ye need to know.*

John Keats,
"Ode to a Grecian Urn"

THE PACIFIC WAR had ended not too long after the European War. Harry Truman became president after Roosevelt's death, and he ordered the atomic bomb dropped on Japan. It was so devastating that it ended the war right then. So I guess that avenged Pearl Harbor.

By now Maxine and Nod had a new baby sister, Bennie Louise. She was never called that but was known as Cootie, then and now. Eunice had met and married a marine named James Hughes, or Jimmy. Jimmy was from Michigan but fell in love with Iron Mine and decided this was where their home would be. They were staying with us for the time being. He wanted to be a farmer and hunter like Papa. He started out with great gusto, going hunting and trapping with Papa, and when spring came, he planted crops and learned to plow with one of the mules. Tractors weren't so plentiful at that time. Then he decided he wanted to raise chickens on the side and asked Mama how she got hers started. She told him how to gather eggs all laid on the same day. She told him to find a hen that wanted to set, put fresh straw in the nest for her to sit on, and put the eggs under her. He set out for the store and came back with a nice cardboard box, which he carried into the kitchen. When Eunice asked him what he was going to do with the box, he said he was going to put it behind the stove for the hen to hatch his biddies.

"Who ever heard of a hen nest behind the stove?" she asked him.

"Well, it's still cold, and the hen needs to be warm," he said.

After we got through laughing, Mama explained the hen would do fine in the chicken coop, where they'd all been nesting before.

Farming wasn't the only thing Eunice's new husband took an interest in. He also went to Sunday school and church with us. Seeing that the young people in Iron Mine didn't have much of a social life, he soon had organized a group and formed a club. We met and decided it would be a Christmas savings club. Each member would pay fees at the weekly meeting, and come Christmas, the money would be divided evenly among us. We elected officers. Mrs. Annie Hayes's youngest boy Hubert (Big Tom), was an outgoing person like Jimmy, full of energy and bright ideas. He was elected president. Dot Bennett was secretary. I was treasurer, Bertha was vice president, and Jimmy was sergeant at arms. He'd been a sergeant on the rifle range down at Camp Lejeune, and as an ex-marine, he made a good one. Members had to behave in public as well as at meetings. If anyone was reported being seen drunk and cutting up or getting arrested or fighting, they had to pay a fine. We met at each other's homes on Friday nights. After we'd met and discussed club business, we had refreshments and then played cards or some other game.

Iron Mine livened up. We had a Halloween party, a weiner roast for Thanksgiving, and a Christmas party. What with all these activities and farmwork, when spring came, time flew by. After a busy summer of farmwork and club activities, like a trip to the lake and picnics, fund-raisers for our club, including a fish fry at Do-Drop Inn and a barbecue, things started winding down. Sam and the rest of the kids who went to college and high school returned to their studies. Bertha left for Fayetteville State College for a year or two to renew her teacher's certificate. And last but not least, Eunice and Jimmy decided to go to Detroit, his hometown, to work for a while and to save to build a house. They wanted a home of their own, and things were slow here during the winter months. The rest of us kept the club going until Christmas. We had a final meeting and divided up all of the money in the treasury. I had the Christmas party at my house. All of us had bought gifts for each other and put them under the tree. After the meeting, we opened gifts and had refreshments, but no one was of a mind to play cards, so they asked James Wright to sing. He was known to have a good singing voice, so he sang "I'm Dreaming of a White Christmas" and "Sentimental Reasons." Mama's and a few others' eyes were wet, and even Papa looked sad. So that was it. It turned out to be a long cold winter with lots of snow.

Iron Mine was quiet and time passed slowly, but I was peaceful and content just being home among the people I loved most. I'll skip the next few years, because they were much like the ones before.

# 15

# A New Beginning

*Warm golden letters all the tablet fill,*
*Nor lose their luster,*
*Till the heart stands still.*

Daniel Webster,
"A Page More Glowing"

WELL, this is the year of our Lord, nineteen hundred and fifty-
five. I was still in Iron Mine, but living a very different life.
Eunice and Jimmy returned from Detroit and built themselves
a nice brick ranch-style home in Pender County. Bennie and
Frank also built new homes. Bennie's home was a few miles down
the road from Eunice's. Frank built one on the eastern edge of
our farm. Willie and Lucille married and made their home in
Buffalo, New York. Sam and I both married—he to a pretty girl
named Sylvia from North Carolina's western hills, and I to James
Wright, the boy who'd saved Edgar from drowning that long-ago
summer afternoon. Though we came from different regions and
backgrounds, we had some things in common, in particular, our
love for Iron Mine and farm life.

I loved all four of my sisters-in-law; however Lucille (Willie's
wife) and Sylvia (Sam's wife) were more my age, and we had more
in common. While Willie was in college at A&T, Lucille and their

174

two children lived with us in order to be near him. They'd married shortly after his discharge from military service. It was fun having three little ones in the house—Billy and Diane and Red, my little girl. Money was scarce, so Lucille and I got most of our pleasure from our babies, playing with the dogs, and catching a ride with Papa to town whenever we had extra money. We spent it on treats for our children if we could stay in the stores long enough. As always, Papa was in a hurry to get to town and in a hurry to get back to his farming, hunting, or whatever. After tending to his own business, he'd look us up to get in the truck. "I got to go," he'd say.

After we got in, he'd look to be sure we were safely inside the truck, then he'd say he would be right back. He'd take off down

My sister-in-law Lucille.

My eldest daughter Linda ("Red").

the street, and we would see him in busy conversation with someone. He'd finally break away, get the truck started, and then stop
at every wayside store between Wallace and home. He knew
everybody, and they knew him. In fact, my whole family was well
known in the town, with me being the exception.

One warm sunny afternoon Lucille and I were outside with
the kids when Subud and James asked us if we'd like to ride with
them to Wrightsville Beach to pick up my Cousin Janie's husband. "Subud" was a nickname for Robert Henry, another boy
Mama and Papa had taken in. He'd gone down there to do some
fall fishing, and after staying there for a few days, he wanted
someone to come get him. Lu and I looked at each other. I know
our eyes were gleaming with thoughts of a ride to somewhere
other than Wallace. They told us to just hop in, that they would
only be picking Bubba up and coming right back. We needed no

more urging. We just grabbed our baby bottles and an extra diaper and jumped in. The sun was still high, the air balmy, and we were sure we'd be back well before dark.

So we set out, with Lu, the kids, and I in back, looking at everything we passed, laughing and chatting as though we'd never been outside of Iron Mine before. It was fun, and we were as happy as larks. Upon reaching the beach, we saw lots of people, boats, and so on, but no Bubba. The boys got out and went to look for him, but they came back alone. The sun was getting low by this time, and I began to think of home. We headed back. Somewhere between the beach and Wilmington the car began acting up a bit. Subud had to stop and tinker with it. In the back seat, Lucille, the kids, and I were much quieter. The boys tinkered, the car started, traveled a few feet, and stopped again. By now it was definitely dark, and a big fall moon was rising. The air had turned quite chilly. We'd only brought one diaper apiece for our babies. We were trying to hold off changing them as long as we could, but knowing they were cold as well as wet, we went on and changed them, hoping they'd stay dry until we got home. I think the car was also out of gas. By now I'd stopped asking what was wrong with it, but just hoped desperately it would get going and not stop until we got home.

At long last, it started moving again. We were too cold to laugh and play on the way back. Home had never looked so good or the wood heater so warm and comforting as it did that night. However, we weren't prepared for the uproar that greeted us. No one had been home when we left, and thinking we'd be right back, we hadn't bothered to leave a note, so no one had any idea where Lucille and I had gone to with our little kids. They knew we couldn't drive and that we never got far from home. Papa was walking the floor and fussing up a storm. It got worse when he saw us. He wanted to know where the devil we'd been with those poor little children. Lu and I could have stayed away, but he felt sorry for the babies. He told us how crazy we were and that he already knew I was crazy but thought Lucille had better sense. I never knew when Bubba came home, but it sure wasn't with us.

This was also the period of time when I lost the dearest friend I have ever had or will have, my mom. She was sick for a little over a year, and it makes me feel better to know I was always there for her. I kept her clean and comfortable. I had three little girls then, Linda (Red), Mary Elizabeth, and Carolyn, the baby. During the day while I cooked, cleaned, and did laundry or whatever, they played near Mama's bed or wheelchair, keeping an eye on her so they could come get me if she needed anything before I got back to her. Papa and James would be home at night, and Papa was there to do for her if she needed anything after I settled her down for the night and went to bed. One Sunday morning in March, Jimmy came over. He had me help her get dressed and took her over to their house to spend the day and have dinner. When he brought her back that evening, she was happy and said she'd had a good time. However, she seemed sort of tired and quiet and went to sleep early. She grew even quieter through the week, and I noticed changes in her. She didn't pass water as she had been doing. I asked Papa to call the doctor to come check on her. He came on Thursday but didn't say much. Eunice came over Friday morning and took breakfast to her, but she couldn't eat it.

While I was doing the dishes, Mama sent for me. Papa was in the room. She asked him to stand by her bed between me and my sister and hold our hands. That done, she looked at the three of us a long time, then told Papa to promise to look out for her two girls as long as he lived, to repair her old home (Grandma's house) and give it to me and not to put another woman over me as long as I was living in our present home. He promised sol-

Mama's grandchildren on her last Mother's Day.

emnly. She was satisfied and fell asleep. We got through Saturday night. Sunday morning, Willie, Lucille, and their children arrived. She was glad to see them, and asked me to give her a sip of water and fix her pillows. After I'd done so, she smiled up at me and signed "I love you." Bending down, I kissed her and said, "I love you too." She went to sleep then and slept all day. About dark, Jimmy came over to see her, then asked me if I'd like to ride over to his house and see his mom, who was down from Detroit for a visit.

He talked about Mama all the way, about how good she was, and that if she didn't make it, I mustn't grieve too hard, but to try to be the same kind of mother to my little girls as she'd been to me. I tried not to even think of not having her in my life, but

when we returned, she had just passed on. Her kidneys had just
stopped working altogether. I guess I went a little crazy. After all
these years it still brings a sharp sadness when I remember that
night and the next few days. Sam took me for a drive to his wife's
home the next day; that helped. Getting through the funeral was
a nightmare. Having my little girls to care for and prayers to my
Lord for help and strength brought me through. When she could
find the time, Eunice came over and took me and the girls to
spend the day with her. When she'd bring me back late in the
afternoon, James would always be sitting right where I'd see him
first thing. That was also a help.

True to his word, Papa and his friend Johnny Rhodes started
work on my grandma's house, as he'd promised Mama he would.
I stayed busy about the house. Sometimes Dorothy, Cap's daughter, would come out to see me and also Jean Harold, one of
Bertha's children. And Annie Mott came with Lattice sometimes.
It was summer by now, and a busy time, so no one had much time
to visit. I still cooked for whoever wanted dinner. But it was so
different from past summers. No one seemed to want to talk, let
alone laugh. They just went about the business of getting their
food inside of them and getting out. Mama's absence was keenly
felt. Often there would be no one for the noon meal but Papa,
me, and my little girls, Red and Mary, unless James was home.
One such day Papa was eating and listening to a nearby radio
when all of a sudden he got up and quickly left the table. I followed, thinking he might be sick. Instead I found him standing
at the foot of Mama's bed, holding on and crying like a child. The
girls came running, and we all held each other in a bunch and
cried together. Red later told me someone on the radio had
started singing a church song Mama had often sung while working about the house. I wish so much that people didn't have to
die.

This was the summer Sam and Sylvia took me and the girls to visit Willie and Lucille. I guess they were trying to get my mind off my loss. I'd never been as far north as Buffalo, New York. We traveled through western Pennsylvania, and when I first saw the mountains I was so thrilled, I got goose bumps. I just couldn't believe it when we were so high up and along came a thundershower. I could see clouds and lightning below me as well as overhead. While there, we went across the border into Canada. That was also very exciting.

At one point I was just about frightened out of my wits. The car stopped at a bridge, and I was busy looking at the beautiful scenery around me. I didn't notice what was going on until all at once a strange White man's face was just inches from mine, and he appeared to be barking, "What's your name?" And before I could answer, he asked, "Where were you born?" Everything I knew flew out the window. I stared at Willie and Lucille while they told me again what he said. I repeated his questions, "What is my name, where was I born?" I frowned and tried to think. I finally got up the presence of mind to say Mary Wright and North Carolina. The face disappeared, and we went on our way. That day I rode on the highest and biggest roller coaster I'd ever seen. Bennie's daughter, Dot, had come with us. She rode with Sam and almost fainted. One night we also went for a ride up the river on a pleasure boat. Next day we visited Niagara Falls. No one had to tell me which was Rainbow Falls and which was Horseshoe. It was all so beautiful, it didn't seem real. We could only stay a couple of days, but I really enjoyed all the beautiful things and places I saw.

By now it was late August. Papa and Mr. Johnny had been working steadily on the house in their spare time, and it was shaping up nicely. I started making new curtains and other things. However, when I thought about leaving my childhood home,

I had mixed feelings. On the one hand, I was excited about having my own home with just my own little family, and I knew it would be better for Red to be where she could get on and off the school bus right in front of the house. On the other, I felt I would be leaving my mom behind and, in some way, my sister and brothers as well, even though I didn't see as much of them. They were all busy trying to deal with their own lives and families. Besides, It was probably distressing for them to see the place where they'd grown up and not find Mama there. Frank came down every so often to see Papa about something and I guess to see if we were all right. He'd usually look in on the girls and play a little. He'd given them names. Linda was "Red," because she had red hair when she was born. Mary was "Bull," and Carolyn was "Little Bull." I doubt he ever knew their real names. Eunice had two large chicken houses to oversee. She and Jimmy sold crates of eggs and fryers. Bennie came for me and the girls to go spend a weekend with him and Mable a couple of times, but I missed the family dinners at home and all the kids running about.

The day finally came when Papa told me to get my things together so he could move us, and he said I could take anything in the house that I wanted except the large pictures of Mama and his boys. James had bought new furniture for our home, so all I took were dishes, bedclothes, and some of Mama's clothes. I cried the whole while. I was also sad that Mr. Richard Thompson was being buried the same day. It worried me when any of my neighbors passed. They were all a part of Iron Mine; besides, he'd always been nice to me, smiling and speaking, and I'd spent many nights with his daughter Caroline.

The move was very exciting for Red and Mary. Carolyn was too young to know the difference. Our first night we were alone. James was on a construction job in Jacksonville and came home weekends. I was sure I would be terrified and decided I'd sit up and read all night. After I'd cooked my children's first dinner in their new home, we sat on the porch and watched people and traffic pass. This, too, was new to them. The road passing our old home also led to Highway 41, but few people used it. We seldom saw people passing. After bathing the girls and getting them ready for bed, I sat on the side of their bed and told them an old-timey tale like I used to love. Soon they were fast asleep. I settled near Carolyn's crib with book and started reading. I'd stop every now and then and look around. Once I went in another room where I could look out the window and see down home. The porch light was on, and a light was in the dining room window. I could just see all of us sitting at the table eating supper and talking over the day, and now Papa was down there all alone, unless Mr. Johnny was with him. My throat and eyes filled up, so I went back to my reading, but I couldn't keep my mind on the story. Then I started dozing and finally decided to go on to bed. I moved the baby's crib close beside my bed, said my prayers, and lay down. I still didn't think I'd sleep. I'd heard so much about this old house being haunted. I looked around me at the room. The light was low, and everything looked so cozy, and I felt so peaceful. I thought about my mom's family who'd lived here and loved each other. It seemed like they were all there in the room, telling me they were watching over me and my babies and not to be afraid. I felt real peaceful and drifted off to sleep and slept straight through the night, as did the children.

Waking at daybreak, I helped Red get dressed for school. She looked so cute in her little starched cotton dress with matching hair bows and socks. While she ate breakfast, I packed her lunch, then stood with her on the porch to wait for her bus. It was so good she didn't have to walk from down home. Our house was on a curve. You could look straight ahead all the way to the highway and see the church and the old schoolhouse. To the left the

road curved north past Mrs. Sissy Maybanks, Miss Lizzie, and her
sister Artelia. Across the road and a field was Frank and Lattice's
house, along with several more homes belonging to Cousin Helen
Boney and her sons, William and Albert Henry; the little church
we kids used to follow Mr. Miller to when he'd have Sunday
evening services; and Cousin Bert Williams's house. I'd known
all these folks since childhood, and now here I was living right
among them. It was all so new.

After the bus had stopped to pick Red up, I went back inside
to see about my other two babies. Mary was awake and sucking
her thumb and wanted to know where Red was. I told her she
had gone to school. After getting her dressed, I fixed our breakfast. I was ready to bathe and dress Carolyn after she woke up.
After feeding her and wrapping her up good, I set out down the
road to my old home with her and Mary. The dogs were happy
to see us coming and came down to meet and walk with us back
to the house. Papa had stopped and given me the key to get in.
Opening the door and walking into the very quiet and empty
house that had always been full of people and noise was hard to
do and felt unreal too—more like I was dreaming. I fixed a place
to lay my baby down, and then with Mary at my heels, I walked
over the house. The saddest place was Mama and Papa's room.
He still slept in the same room as he had done with Mama for
over forty years. I'd packed up her personal things and given
them away, but the room still seemed to hold something of her
in it. I made the bed and tidied up, swept the floors, and found
something to cook for Papa's dinner. While that was cooking, I
washed his clothes and then sat on the porch and talked to the
dogs and played with Mary. We called her "Cookie." Finally
dinner was done, and there was nothing more for me to do, so I
got my babies ready and walked back to my new home. It felt
good to unlock my own door and smell the newness and see the

cheerful look. I felt less lonely. It was almost time for the school bus, so I put on my own dinner. Cookie sat on the porch so she could see the bus stop and Red get off.

This was a Friday and James came home that evening, so I had all of my little family for dinner. He was pleased with the house and said he wouldn't be going back to Jacksonville. He didn't want me and the children there alone and would find work closer home.

And so life settled into a new pattern, so different from the past few years. Each day I got Red off to school and fixed James breakfast before he left for work. Then after morning chores I set out for down home to do the same for Papa. He was usually out and gone by the time I got there. By now it was early fall, and crops such as sweet potatoes and corn had to be gathered, and cotton, if he had any. I picked whatever vegetables were left in the garden and some of Mama's fall flowers. Sometimes on the way back to my house I would go across the field to the grape arbor Sam and I had once played under and picked the sweet-smelling grapes. Across the road in front of my house I noticed some really beautiful young trees. One was bright red, the other was a lovely shade of yellow, and then there was a gold and russet. I couldn't help going to see what they were. They turned out to be sassafras, gum, dogwood, and oak. Life was good again.

# 16

# *Hurricane Hazel*

*Let me live in a house by the side of the road*
*Where the race of men go by*
*The men who are good, the men who are bad*
*As good and as bad as I.*

Sam Walter Foss,
"House by the Side of the Road"

ONE MORNING after I'd just come back from down home, the
school bus came back and let Red off. Surprised, I asked why
they'd let school out so early. She didn't know exactly, but said
someone had said something about a storm. Looking at the sky,
I saw it was clouding up. Not long afterward James came in, and
it started to rain a little, then the wind picked up. Pretty soon it
was raining harder, and the wind was getting stronger, but there
was no thunder or lightning. Two of the dogs had followed me
home—Lady, and Mama's dog, Tarzan. We let them in and closed
the windows and doors. By now the wind was really strong and
blew some of my porch flowers across the yard. I yelled for James
to catch them. He tried, but every time he stooped to pick one
up, the wind blew it farther away. When I looked again, the flower
pot was heading across the ditch and the field with James right
behind it. I screamed for him to let it go and come back to the

house. He caught up with one and returned to the house, battling the strong wind all the way.

We all settled down in one room, waiting for the storm to pass over, but it only grew stronger instead. Rain was pouring down in white sheets, and the wind was a howling gale, but still I didn't see any lightning or feel the boom of thunder. I remarked to James that I'd never seen a storm like this before. I went into another room to try to see down home, praying Papa was all right. I couldn't see anything at all except that the ground under the window was really deep with water and the house began to shudder at times.

I was growing worried about the strange weather but didn't want the children to know. I placed three chairs in a row and sat down with Carolyn in my lap and the other two on each side. I told them the story of Noah and the Ark and how God took care of them and let the Ark float on the water as it rose. Then I sung to them. I never was much of a singer, even when I could hear, so I know I must have sounded frightful, but my babies seemed to like it and stopped being scared. Finally Carol went to sleep, and I took her back in the room where James was and laid her down, then told Red and Mary to let's all lie down. When I looked out the window again, small pieces of debris were flying by, and they asked me what it was. I said I didn't know, but let's pretend it was snowing. They liked that game too and soon fell asleep smiling.

James told me to come in the kitchen and look out the window. Trees were falling across the road one after the other. Some of the debris I had seen was pieces of the roof, and now the ceiling began to leak. We put buckets, pans, and washtubs over the floor to catch the water. The wind was blowing with a fury. I went back to the bed where my little girls lay and decided there was nothing I could do. So I lay down beside them, said a prayer, and

decided if God was ready for me I was ready also, and my babies
were innocent and he'd take care of them. I felt calm and peaceful then and went on to sleep. When I woke up again, it was late
evening. The storm had stopped. The sun was shining, and our
whole yard looked like a lake. The shelves in our kitchen had
been shaken down, and a lot of decorative dishes lay broken.
Some had been my Mama's. But we were all unhurt, and the only
serious damage to the house was to the roof. So I was very thankful. My papa came wading through the water with his hip boots
on to see if we were okay. That's when I found out this had been
a hurricane, Hurricane Hazel of 1954.

He said he had heard on the radio that it had done a lot of
damage on the beaches and elsewhere; people had been killed.
I saw how blessed we had been. It also touched my heart that
Papa had waded through all of that water to make sure we'd come
through unharmed. Eunice and Sylvia came over the next day to
see us too. They asked me if I'd been afraid. I said I was a little
at first, but then I decided if God was ready for me, I was ready
to go and lay down with my babies and went to sleep. They stared
at me and then looked at each other. They never said what they
were thinking, so I wondered if they thought I was crazy or what.
Even though there have been lots of hurricanes since then,
people still talk about Hurricane Hazel. It was said that only three
houses were left standing on Carolina Beach.

My days settled into a steady routine of taking care of both
places. One day Papa came in while I was down home. He had a
catalog and told me to come sit down and look at it with him. It
turned out go be a catalog of headstones for graves. He wanted
me to help him choose one for Mama's grave and decide what to
have engraved on it. We went back and forth. At first he wanted
a double stone with his name on one side, but it was too expensive, so we finally picked a nice, but less costly, one. On the grave-

stone he put her name and that she was his wife. Then he put, "She believeth and sleeps in Jesus." He wiped his eyes and told me he wanted to be buried right beside her when his time came. Then we picked three more gravestones, two for her parents, and one for her oldest brother, Buddy Vatson. All the members of her family are buried in a row beside each other except her sister, Sis Ett. She's a little farther over, next to her husband.

Red took to schooling. Every day she came hurrying in all excited about something new she had learned and the letters she had printed in her tablet. Her teacher was my cousin James Thompson's wife, Thelma. She'd made many new friends and could fingerspell their names. I'd wash, starch, and iron all of her little cotton dresses. She liked hearing them rustle and called them her paper dresses. Girls didn't wear pants and jeans to school then. They had to wear leather shoes, socks, and dresses or skirts and blouses. I also joined the PTA. The other parents in the neighborhood were happy to pick me up to ride with them. Melissa and her husband, Albert Boney, would let me ride with them; also, Ed Wallace and his wife, Amy, and Elmo and his wife, Hattie Pearl, would give me a ride. However, we soon settled on Hattie Pearl as our regular driver. Each one of us gave her change for gas. The men all worked during the day and disliked having to drive at night when they were tired.

One day Red came home and told me that the next night would be PTA and the teachers wanted all of the parents to bring a cake or pie for their play. I asked her what would they do with the cakes and pies. She didn't know, but she guessed the children would eat them. "Oh well," I thought, "that would be easy enough." I liked baking cakes, and I'd always been told they were good. The only problem was the next day when I looked over my shelves, there wasn't anything for icing, and I didn't have any way to get to town to buy anything before it would be time to go. I

had some nice apples and decided to make a pie. The first pie
looked perfect when I took it out of the oven, so I decided to
make a smaller one for my children's supper. The crust burnt a
little, but I knew I could trim it off. I let them cool while I got
dressed. When I went to take the best pie out of the pan, the
crust stuck in one place, and when I tried to loosen it up, the rest
of it split and crumbled. Oh great! What would I do now? No time
to make another. But I wanted to carry something. After all, I took
being the parent of a schoolchild seriously and wanted to do my
part. My eyes fell on the small pie with the burnt crust, and I
thought, since it's for the kids to eat I could trim it off and wrap
it up. I envisioned the children gathered around a table having a
tea party.

Melissa hadn't had time to make a cake either, so she stopped
at a small store on the way to the school and brought a ready-
made pound cake. When we were seated in the auditorium, some
of the older girls went around collecting our donations, which
were carried someplace up front. Our PTA president, Mrs. Yottie
Teachey, called the meeting to order. That done, the children put
on a brief program of songs and speeches. Then I looked for them
to gather for their tea party. Instead, to my horror and great surprise they brought out the cakes and pies, setting them in rows
across the edge of the stage, unwrapped! There were such beautiful cakes and perfect meringue pies. I saw Melissa's little cake
placed on the end of the row with my raggedy pie next to it. Then
to my horror a man went up and selected a beautiful cake and
started auctioning it off. It sold quickly for about five dollars.
Others went for more or less, but all sold well until they were all
gone except my and Melissa's offerings. Then my pie was picked
up and passed around under people's noses with the question
"What bid will I get for this?" He didn't call it anything. Silence.
No one wanted it, and they passed it in front of me. I refused to

recognize my handiwork, I just stared ahead. Finally some man looked at it and said he didn't know what it was, but he'd take it for seventy-five cents. No one protested, so it was sold. Next, Melissa's cake was passed around. It went for fifty cents. Oh well, the school was richer by $1.25 due to our efforts. From then on I made sure I kept in close contact with the teachers at Teachey Elementary School, so I would know beforehand exactly what was expected of me.

Life settled into a very different pattern from the past few years. But I was often reminded of it by my little girls. After they'd had baths and dressed for bed, we had Bible reading, and then each one got to name a story they wanted to hear. Sometimes they'd rather me tell them about when I was a little girl and about things they did themselves that they couldn't remember. Red liked to hear about one night when she, Mama, and I were alone and she found a marble and tried to eat it. She sat on the floor, eyes bulging, when Mama snatched her up and started trying to dislodge it. I panicked and flew out the door minus a coat or shoes, even though it was a cold winter night. I headed for Frank's house to get help. He lived all the way across our farm near the highway. I hardly felt the cold ground as I ran. All I could think was that my baby was choking to death, and I had to get help for her.

I burst through Frank's kitchen door. He'd already heard me running and was out of his chair coming to meet me. I gasped out that Red was choking, and he started for the door just as barefoot as I was. It happened that Bennie and Mable had come for a visit and said they'd drive me back home to get Red and Mama. Although Bennie went as fast as he could over the ruts and mud holes, it seemed to take forever. Once again I burst through the door expecting to find my child out cold or dead. Instead she was sitting on Mama's lap munching on a cookie while Mama combed and braided her hair. It seemed after I left, Mama had turned her upside down and patted her back. The marble had dropped out. The crisis was over, and my baby was fine, thanks to the good Lord and my mom.

Mary also liked to hear about her scary time. She was even younger, only a few days old. Babies were still a fairly new experience for me on my own. Mama had gone to Frank's house for a visit since James would be around the house with me. I was sitting by the fire feeding her and feeling drowsy and content while James listened to the radio. All at once I became aware that Mary was very still and I couldn't feel her breathing. I looked more closely and saw that her eyes were closed and her little face seemed puffy. I moved her hands, and they seemed limp. The only thing I could think of was that she had choked while I was feeding her and that she was dying. I jumped up and told James something was wrong with the baby. He came running and took her out of my arms, smoothing her hair and blowing in her face. I screamed for him to go call Dr. Blair. He set out running while I held and rocked her. Still no response. I went on the porch and screamed for him to come back, that my poor baby was dead. Poor James ran back, snatching her out of my arms again, stroking and blowing. By now Red was awake and screaming too, not even knowing what for. I snatched her back again. That time I looked at her and her eyes were open and she was smiling. About that time Mama came in wanting to know what was the matter. Upon hearing our fearful story, she took the baby, sat down, examined her, and found nothing wrong. She said I'd probably fed her too long and she'd fallen asleep without being burped. My mom gave me many lessons on the proper care of a baby. I never forgot them, and that never happened again. I'm very thankful Mama was here to help me with my first two.

I'm also glad I made the decision to move back home when I did. Not long before she died, Mama told me I had made her very happy during the past ten years by being there and sharing my little girls with her. She dearly loved the grandchildren she had by her sons but had always wanted some by her daughters as well. It sort of made up for the years I'd been away from my family. I was also grateful I'd been there to care for her and keep her comfortable through her final days.

My four girls: Carol, Linda, Judy, and Mary.

# 17

## Ups and Downs

DIFFERENT PEOPLE have been curious as to how I managed to raise my children and care for them without being able to hear, and they have asked me about it. I never thought much about it at the time, but looking back, I think it was due to Mama's teaching and the instinct God gave me to sense what I couldn't hear, because I could always tell when one of my babies needed me, day or night. I've never been able to figure out why some hearing people think that if a person loses her hearing she loses her mind and feelings as well. We have all of the feelings, hopes, and dreams as anyone else, maybe more than some. My children are the center of my life and my purpose for living. Every day I thank God for placing them in my care, and no matter how old they get, they are still my babies.

Back to their growing-up years, one morning I saw Papa pass in the truck dressed in his Sunday clothes. He didn't stop, so I wondered where he was headed. I thought he might be going to a convention at some church or to something the Masons he belonged to were having. I didn't see him come home all day, but sometime after dark, I was in the kitchen cleaning up the supper dishes when he walked in grinning a little. I smiled back and asked where he'd been all day and if he was all right.

He looked around a while then looked at me and said, "I went and got married."

My mouth hung open, but then my brain started working again, and I asked, "Who?"

It was Bertha's mother, Mrs. Sally. I told him I hoped he'd be happy again and hugged him. He cried and patted my head and went out.

"Well," I thought, "Papa won't be down there alone." I didn't want him to spend the rest of his life lonely and sad. I wished him well, and after that I didn't go down home every day anymore.

I still liked to walk someplace, so I took Mary and Carolyn and walked across the field to Frank and Lattice's house to visit if they were home, or to some of the other neighbors I hadn't seen much of—Mrs. Lizzy and her sister, Artelia, Sadie Murphy, Annie Mott, Cousin Helen Boney, and Mrs. Sissie Maybanks—or I just walked along the woods enjoying the outdoors. Red would be in school. Edna had come back from Philadelphia and married her high school love, but they now lived with Aunt Mary and Uncle Tom just across the woods. She had two little girls, Lorey and Shelia. We started visiting each other often. Our children enjoyed playing together, and she and I loved to talk and read romance magazines and discuss the stories while drinking coffee.

It was about this time that Edna, Mrs. Bertha Williamson (better known as Cousin Bert Williams), and Sam's wife, Sylvia, started playing a big part in our lives. Cousin Bert lived in the same little house across the field that her sister Cousin Honlow had lived in years ago, the house where she made tea cakes for

Sam and me when we played in her back yard under a pear tree
while Mama worked nearby. They were both short in stature,
round, and a little stooped. They liked to wear long dresses and
long full aprons, and they always had something on their heads,
either a scarf or an old hat. Cousin Honlow had been a sweet kind
little lady. The winter I was taking treatment for my eyes and
couldn't go to school, you would see her coming down the road
with her little black iron pot filled with dry field peas she'd
cooked for me because I loved them so good. It was a blow to
come home one spring and find out she'd fallen sick and died.
Now her sister had moved in her house, but Cousin Bert was as
different from her sister as night and day. There was no sweet-
talking from Cousin Bert. She could fix her eyes on you and make
you squirm, and could outargue anybody. You wanted to avoid
getting into a hassle with her. Anyone who displeased her was "an
old brute." However, if she liked you, she was truly your friend.
As I mentioned earlier, she'd walk all the way down home to see
Mama while she was sick when her own rheumatism was so painful she'd have to crawl up the steps coming in. Now she walked
over to my house most days and sat on the porch with her snuffbox, watching everybody who passed.

Sam and Sylvia had built a nice little house next door to
Eunice, and both were teaching at Bland Elementary School in
Sampson County. They had a little girl Mary's age, Bonita. Sylvia
often brought her over to play with my girls. Sometimes they'd
spend the night. Cousin Bert had also taken to spending the night
at my house. She said she used to visit there when my mom's
family lived there. She was friends with one of my aunts, Duella.
I tell you about these people because I want you to get to know
who they are. They played an important part in my life, and I will
mention them often.

Red was enjoying school and making good progress. I attended PTA every time they had it and met many of the teachers and other parents. Red made sure she brought all of her friends, both girls and boys, to meet me.

My sister-in-law, Sylvia.

# 18

# Holidays without Mama

IT WAS nearing Thanksgiving, and I was wondering how I'd deal with it, and also with Christmas. It was the first holiday without Mama, and I'd have only my little family to cook and plan for, when I'd been doing it for a crowd, not to mention the empty place that had been Mama's. I decided I would go on and cook a big dinner anyway. I still had folk, and I didn't feel they'd forget me entirely. James brought home a large turkey, and I got vegetables together and baked sweet potato pies and a cake. Red and Mary helped me rake the yard and burn leaves and trash. At least Red was a help. Mary tried, and some of the little boys who lived nearby gave a hand when they passed by. I baked the turkey late that night after my babies were in bed, as the pies and cakes had been baked earlier. I sat in the kitchen and read while good smells filled the air. Next morning after breakfast James announced he was going to help Jimmy harvest a field of corn he had nearby. He was bringing some of the guys from Cross Road to help him also. I told him okay, but to be sure to come in for dinner.

"Are we having company?" he asked.

I didn't know for sure, but I took for granted that some of my family would come by. They'd always seemed to enjoy the dinner

Mama and I cooked down home in past years. So I cooked busily and happily through the day. I saw bird hunters going by to go hunting with Papa. That was another Thanksgiving tradition. Some of them used to eat with us too. Mama always made them welcome. I wondered if they'd miss her this year. I believed they would. These were from Greensboro, well-to-do businessmen. One was Mr. Venning, and the other one was Mr. Forbis. He owned a funeral home business. I wasn't sure what the others did, but they all seemed nice and had sent cards and money when Mama died.

After all the food was cooked and keeping warm, I combed the children's hair and put fresh clothes on them. I wanted things to be nice. We set the table using Mama's best tablecloth and the pretty china she'd given me the last Christmas she was able to shop. Then we sat and waited. No one came. Frank's two little boys, Duke and Jimrod, passed by waving and said, "Hey, Aunt Mary," on their way down home to see Billy, their little cousin from Buffalo who'd come for Thanksgiving. The dinner hour passed, and still I'd seen no one.

My children's stomachs were empty, and they were asking, "When do we eat?"

I told them in a little bit. I went on the porch one more time to look. This time I saw Jimmy's truck heading for the house with all his dusty helpers. He was coming to bring James home for dinner, but he always came in to speak and see if I had anything good to eat. When he saw the table, he asked who my company would be.

"No one, it seems," I told him.

He and James both knew my feelings well. They looked at each other and then asked if I'd like to have dinner guests.

I knew what they were thinking so I said, "Sure thing, tell the boys to come in and wash up."

Jimmy took soap, water, and towels out and the boys washed and dusted themselves as best they could and in came my Thanksgiving company. There was Lattice's brother, Carl Henry, her cousin, Marvin, and his brother Vatin and a few more. I got busy putting food on the table, and all gathered around. It did my heart good to see that food going down, apparently enjoyed. When all had finished and got up to leave, each one came and said how much they enjoyed their dinner and thanked me; some shook hands. James and Jimmy grinned. I knew Eunice would have another meal waiting for him when he got home. I was reminded of the Bible story of the man who'd prepared a big feast for some special people and they didn't come, so he'd sent his servants out to invite who ever was on the streets. Well, I knew how that was and I was happy.

Thanksgiving passed, and soon Christmas was upon us. There was a program at the schoolhouse before school closed for the holidays. Sylvia came to take me and the children. Red had a speech to recite and the children gathered around the old upright piano to sing Christmas songs while Miss Wallace played for them. She was the fourth grade teacher. They also received Christmas bags of fruit and candy. The week before Christmas I did my usual baking of cakes and pies as I'd done down home, the same kind, chocolate, pineapple, coconut, raisin and jelly cake. I also cooked sweet potato pies. They sat in a row, wrapped and waiting for Santa to come sample them on Christmas Eve night.

I'll always remember that first Christmas in my new home. It was a mixture of feelings, pride and happiness at being in my own home and having things ready for my little ones. I'd cleaned the house from one end to the other. It smelled fresh and scrubbed, the windows clear and sparkling with the pine scent of the tree. But there was sadness too. The memory of past Christmases and family were with me too.

After I'd put the children to bed and finished the last of my cooking, there was no more to be done. I tried to read but couldn't concentrate. James was out with his pals someplace. He had promised to be in to help me get the children's toys set up. I sat looking in the fireplace thinking of how it had once warmed my own mother when she was a child and lived here. Trying to imagine how she'd looked and what she and her sisters and brothers got for their Christmas gifts. That had been back in the 1800s. Then all my loneliness came over me at once, and I cried. Afterward, I felt better and was okay by the time James came in. We set out everything, then I sliced him a piece of each cake, ate some myself, and we went to bed.

Seems we'd hardly closed our eyes when little hands patted us awake again. They'd smelled their goodies, got up and found dolls, strollers, treats and other things to make them happy. So, James and I had to share their joy and be surprised, too. They also had to go view each cake with a slice missing and find further proof the jolly old elf had indeed been to visit them. We had breakfast, then they set about playing in earnest. Edna walked over with her kids clutching their new dolls, that had to be shown off and admired also. Later, Eunice came over to bring us the nice gifts she always had and asked us to go over to her house and eat with her sometime during the holidays. Lattice sent what she had for us. Since she and I both had a bunch of children and not too much money we always tried to get things the children could use like, socks, hair bows, undies, etc. And for each other it would be a bowl, bread pan, dish towels and such. Sam and Sylvia also brought nice gifts for us. Bennie and Mable usually managed to get up and bring something good from their farm. Papa could enjoy his Christmas as well since he was no longer down there alone, so we were all blessed with a good season.

# 19

# Cousin Bert

*Like music heard on the waters*
*Like pines when the wind passeth by*
*Like pearls in the depth of the ocean*
*Like stars that enamel the sky.*

A. P. Stanley

THE HOLIDAYS were past, and once again life settled back into a routine, with the usual after-Christmas letdown and bad weather.

One night Cousin Bert Williams had come over to spend the night. She often did that now. Toward evening she could be seen coming along a path across the field with a white bag containing her gown and whatever else she carried in there, along with her handbag and snuffbox. Sometimes she'd have the makings for a cake and bake it in my kitchen while she sat before the fireplace with her shoes off warming her feet and talking with whoever would talk with her. She liked nothing better than having a good argument with someone and calling them an old brute.

This particular night I was getting the girls ready for bed. When I started on Carolyn, I noticed Cousin Bert was looking at Carolyn and listening to her breathing. "Don't that baby have a cold?" she asked me.

"Yes ma'am," I told her.

"What are you giving her for it?" I started naming the different baby medicines I had.

For each one named, she said, "Humph."

She sat and thought a while longer then started putting on her stockings and shoes. After I'd laid the baby down she told me to put on my shoes and coat too.

"Why?" I asked her.

"You're going with me over to my house to get something for that cold."

I knew James could look out for the children, so I got dressed to go with her. When we were ready to go, I opened the door to the porch. It was pitch black outside.

"Get a flashlight," I was told.

"I don't have one," I said.

That didn't faze Cousin Bert. She picked up a piece of kindling by the fireplace known as a lightwood knot, lit it in the fireplace, and told me to come on. We held on to each other and followed the road to Miss Sissie Maybank's house as best we could. The dirt road was soft and slippery with mud from the rain we'd had earlier. Turning off by Miss Sissie's yard, we took a path across the field to Cousin Bert's house.

Once inside, she lit an oil lamp and went about the rooms collecting different things and handing them to me to carry. One was a little black iron pan. Finally satisfied, she said, "Let's go," and blew out the light, and we headed for her front door. She directed me to follow the path in front of her house this time. She thought it would be less muddy, I guess. All went well with our hissing and flickering torch until we reached the end of the path and met with a board crossing the ditch. Here disaster struck. We tried crossing the board together, but it wasn't wide enough. We tried one going ahead while the other held on to her coattail.

We couldn't hold on well because we both had bags, bottles, and torches to carry. This made us very unsteady. I inched ahead because I had the torch to light our way. She had a hold on my back someplace. Upon reaching the middle of our bridge, it started to wobble and shake. Next thing we knew, we were both down in the ditch all tangled up. It was a shallow ditch but still held enough water to douse our torch, and we were left in complete blackness. I could feel Cousin Bert's voice and knew she was doing some fussing. But I couldn't hear her words, so whatever she was saying didn't bother me.

We finally got untangled and out of the ditch and back on our way again minus our light. Our feet felt their way homeward bit by bit. Fortunately this was a shorter route so it wasn't long before we walked through my door again—two muddy and messed-up women. After getting cleaned up, Cousin Bert set about cooking up her cold remedy. By some miracle, we hadn't lost anything. After ordering James to build up the fire in the fireplace, she sat her little black pot on a bed of coals with her chair in front of it and a long-handled spoon. My job was to fetch and carry. First, red root onions were chopped and fried, then a little water was added. After that, I don't know what went in the pot. I think some mutton salve and other things. It smelled terrible. James left the house. She stirred and hummed. When the mixture had finally cooked to her satisfaction, she pulled the pot off the coals to cool down a bit. After it was ready, she looked at me and said, "Bring me that baby." I went and got my precious baby and placed her in Cousin Bert's lap, but stood by ready to snatch her back if anything looked wrong. She undressed Carolyn, then had me spread a soft blanket over her lap, laid Carolyn on it, and proceeded to grease every inch of her from head to toe with the bad-smelling mixture in her pot. I had to warm up pieces of white flannel and another blanket. When she used up all of the concoction, she spread the flannel over her chest and back and replaced her sleepers and wrapped her in the warm blanket, rocked and hummed to her awhile longer, then gave her back to me to lay her in her crib. The baby was asleep and slept and breathed easy all through the night. No coughing or crying.

I tried to thank Cousin Bert before she left the next morning, but all she'd say was "Humph."

# 20

# *So, the Winter Is Past and Gone*

*For lo, the winter is past,*
*The rain is over and gone,*
*The flowers appear on the earth,*
*The time of the singing of birds have come.*

Book of Solomon,
"Song of Songs"

SPRING WAS budding again. Maple trees taking on a reddish hue. The daffodils Papa had planted on Mama's and his little boy Bud's graves were blooming in profusion. Sometimes I rode to the cemetery with Papa, and we'd weed and work around the graves. Other times I'd walk with the children and show them the graves of various uncles, aunts, and great-grandparents in addition to Mama's. They'd ask so many questions about their dead relatives. In any case they learned about death and people dying and took it all in stride.

Edna and I had more time together now that the days were longer. Instead of sitting by the fireplace with the coffeepot on, we sat outside under the trees talking and watching our children play. It seems we could never catch up on the years we'd been separated, she in Philadelphia and parts of New York, while I was in D.C. and back home. Sometimes Sylvia would join us. She and Sam had built a small country store right close by. She'd run the store while their little girl played with my children when she wasn't with her Aunt Eunice. Sometimes Cousin Bert would pass by and stop to have her say. She also enjoyed stopping in at Aunt Mary and Uncle Tom's, Edna's grandparents, to have a good argument with Uncle Tom. It was a pleasant and peaceful time.

School was about to close, and Red was all excited about the part she had in the program. She had to learn a speech and say a line in a skit. She insisted on saying it for me over and over whether I heard her or not. I always learned whatever she had to say so I could follow her lips and know whether she really knew it. I dressed her in her best on the big night, and Sylvia came over to drive us to the schoolhouse. I was so proud of my little girl.

Some of the farmers had planted blueberry fields to try a new crop. They'd send old school buses or trucks around to pick up anyone who wanted a job picking the large berries. The women were glad to go pick and make extra money as were a few of the men. They could only use children over twelve for the work. The rows were very long, and the ground was white and sandy, so when the sun grew hot, the sand did too, and with no shade, it was very hot in the fields. However, most of the local women found someone to watch their small kids and took the older ones to pick with them. Some of the children nearby would come over to my house for a while to play with my girls. Sometimes I'd spread something under a tree, make a pitcher of Kool-Aid, and invite them to sit down. My girls would ask me to tell a Timey Tale, so the other children could hear it. After giving out cookies to go with the Kool-Aid, I'd tell the stories I told my children: "The Three Little Pigs," "The Three Bears," "Little Red Riding

Hood," and so on. They loved them all. Time would fly, and they'd have to hurry home before their moms returned.

Now that I was a little closer to the church and my children a little older, I'd started going more often. We still didn't have a car, so sometimes I caught a ride with Papa and Mrs. Sally. More often I walked. I'd get myself and the girls dressed, pack the baby's bag, putting in a pair of dress shoes with heels for myself, and wear an old pair of loafers for walking. Red would hold Mary's hand, while I carried Carolyn. When we reached a large oak tree beside the road near the church, I'd change my walking shoes for heels, hiding the old shoes in a hole in the trunk of the tree, and so tripped into church in style.

We had a new pastor, Reverend Louis Wright. When he found out he had a deaf member, he went out of his way to meet me and my children. Since we had never heard of the church having interpreters for the deaf, and I was the only deaf person around, he'd let me know the text of his sermons and give them to me to read. He and Mrs. Wright often had dinner with Papa. He'd always stop by my house, call the children to the car, and talk with them and, like Papa, leave them with a little change and candy or gum. I grew to like him very much, almost as well as I did Reverend Tim. He and his wife had both died by this time. He did live long enough to preach my Mama's funeral, as she'd asked him to some years before. I'll always be glad of that.

# 21

# *Changes*

*The laugh-with-me-its-funny things*
*And it's the jolly, joking things*
*The "never mind the trouble" things*
*That make the world seem bright.*

Author unknown,
"The Friendly Things"

SOMETIMES when I look back and think about the many changes in my life, it seems that no matter how many changes took place, one thing never did—I always managed to get into some kind of adventure, whether here at home as a child, off at school in Raleigh, in Washington and Arlington, then back home again.

My life now was so very different from what it used to be that sometimes I found it hard to believe this was really me. Every night before going to bed, I'd stand at the window facing down home, looking at the light in the windows and remembering my family. I'd see Mama most of all, then the rest of my family and remember the warm, safe, cozy feeling I'd had going to sleep, knowing all of the people I loved best were right there around me. Now it was very different. Mama was no longer there, and it was hard thinking of someone else in the home that had been hers. At the same time, I knew Papa needed somebody. The rest of us had moved away. I saw more of Frank and Papa than the others did. They stopped by or passed by often. Eunice came by when she could find time, and sometimes I rode to Wallace with her and Lattice. Sam and Sylvia were both still teaching at Bland Elementary.

My new life was full. I was enjoying being a housewife with a school-age child, and after the mishap with the apple pie, I made sure I stayed on top of school and class doings. Red loved school. They now had a lunchroom, and the children could get a free breakfast of oatmeal and milk. Lunch was fifteen cents with a small box of milk, and ten cents without. I sent Red's teacher seventy-five cents every Monday morning to pay for her lunch for the week. One evening she came home with a very upset stomach and had to stay home the next day. I wasn't sure what it was, but she didn't have a fever, so I didn't think it was a virus. James said it was the food and went to Wallace in a snowstorm to see the druggist and get medicine for her. After that, I bought her a lunchbox, and she carried lunch and milk from home.

Most mornings after everybody had gone, I'd be cleaning the kitchen and I'd see Edna coming down the road with her two little girls. I'd stir the fire in my wood kitchen stove and set the coffeepot back on. I was always glad to see her. After getting the kids put down to play, we'd sit by the stove with the coffeepot between us. She'd light a cigarette to go with hers. I never could see what good that would do, so we argued over it. She was a heavy smoker, as was James, and I tried hard to get both of them to quit. I lost the battle, so she smoked, talked, and sipped coffee. Edna had a unique way of talking to me. She'd use her voice and fingerspell at the same time. Every time she'd make a letter, she made it like she was throwing it at me. This amused the children, and they'd laugh. I understood her though and enjoyed her visits. When she would have to go, I'd gather up my kids and walk back with her. There we'd sit in her kitchen while she started dinner for Aunt Mary and Uncle Tom. They always seemed pleased to see me come in with Edna. That became our daily routine. We made a path across the woods so it was quicker to get to and from each other's houses. Sometimes we ventured out and visited the people we didn't often see because they lived beside the highway—Mrs. Annie Hayes, who was Edna's aunt, Cousin Mary Frank, Cousin Bert Lane, and others. Mostly, we enjoyed each other's company and our children. These years, too, were slipping by, so I'll just pick out the highlights in each one.

The year was 1956, and Papa had a heart attack. He'd been bird hunting with Jimmy one afternoon in November when he gave out and had to sit down often. Alarmed, Jimmy asked him what was wrong. He tried to make light of it and said his chest hurt a little. That wasn't like Papa. He could walk for miles without tiring. The next morning Jimmy came over and took him to see our family doctor. It didn't take him long to figure out the problem, and the doctor ordered him to go to the nearest hospital, which was in Wilmington. Papa had to return home first to get ready. When he and Jimmy came back out, I ran on the porch and across the yard to tell him bye, but the car sped on by. So I was left standing there crying. I found out later he was also crying and that they were trying to get him there as fast as they could.

A few days later, James had to take me to Dr. Hawes's clinic for the birth of our fourth and final little one. I'd gotten up that morning feeling out of sorts—depressed and achy, and cranky too. I'd gotten James off to work and Red to school, then sat down in a kitchen chair and cried. That's how Edna found me when she walked in. She knew at once what was wrong. First she made me go lie down for a nap. She finished cleaning my kitchen and made

sure I wasn't in labor. Then she gathered up my laundry, took
Mary and Carolyn along with her kids, and headed back to her
house. Before leaving, she said if I had that baby before she got
back she'd beat me. That was Edna. I don't know what I would
have done without her. She had been coming every day and
helping me with whatever I was doing, and smoking her long
cigarettes and talking crazy to make me laugh. Although our
friendship had many trials, it lasted through the years and always
remained strong. After a peaceful nap and rest, I felt somewhat
better and got up and started dinner.

When Edna came back, she had all my clothes freshly washed
and ironed. It was a good thing she did, because James had to take
me over to Rose Hill to Dr. Hawes's little maternity clinic right
after dinner. Edna had already told me she'd stay with my children along with hers and not to worry about them. I was really
in labor when we reached the clinic, and Dr. Hawes was already
delivering another baby. He was having complications with the
delivery. The nurse gave me a shot to slow things down until Dr.
Hawes could get to me, and poor James was having a hissy fit.
Anyone would have thought he was the patient. It was a cold
rainy night in late November. He was in a hurry to get back to
see about the children, but he didn't want to leave until he was
sure I was okay. A nurse finally came in and took me to a room
to put a gown on me. After I was settled in bed, James tried to
sit and talk, but he couldn't keep still and just prowled around.
He wanted to smoke a cigarette but had nothing to light it with.
The shot they had given me seemed to have slowed things down
too much, because now I was out of pain and felt pretty good.

I told James to go on back home, as it was quite late by now,
sometime between twelve and one, and he had to work the next
day. He didn't care, but finally a nurse helped me convince him
to go home and that I'd be fine. He left shortly before daybreak.

I lay there in bed and everything was quiet. I didn't know it then, but the other girl they'd been working on when I came in had died. Someone came in, and I looked up to find a white girl, who looked about my age, standing there looking at me smiling. She said hi; I answered. She motioned to a chair and asked if she could sit down. I said go ahead. She introduced herself as Faye and said she had come in with a friend but her friend didn't need her now, so she'd sit with me if I wanted company. I was only too glad to have somebody, so we started getting acquainted. She didn't live far from Iron Mine and was also married and had children. Soon one of the nurses came in and also sat down. We talked about different things, including names for babies. They tried to help me pick out a name. They were pretty names, but I'd long ago decided to name my baby Helena if it was a girl and James Dorsett if it was a boy. I was still feeling good, no pains, so the nurse gave me another shot to start my labor again. It didn't, and I started getting drowsy. I'd been awake all night. Day was breaking, so Faye said she had to go home to see about her children. She said for me to keep in touch and to come visit her sometime. I thanked her for staying with me, and she said she'd stop in to see me sometime when she was passing through.

The nurse checked me again and gave me another shot, and then she said it was time for her to go off-duty. Another nurse had come in to take her place. She put a small brass bell beside my bed and said to ring it if I needed anyone. She said she was going to go home and try to sleep, but she knew she wouldn't because her kids would be in and out, slamming doors. She told me good-bye and left. Soon another nurse came in to check me and tell me who she was. It was really day by now, and still no baby, no pain. After the new nurse checked me again, I was given yet another shot and told to ring the bell if my pains started up. I lay there trying to go to sleep and wondering whether this baby would ever get here, when I felt a twinge of pain. It went away, then came another pain. I rang the bell, and no one came, but another pain did, harder this time. I rang the bell again. Still no one came. By now I knew I had to get to the delivery room quick. Since I knew I was just down the hall a bit, I got myself out of bed, still ringing that little bell as hard as I could. They heard it this time, and the nurse and Dr. Hawes were coming behind me with a gurney. I didn't wait for them, and by the time they reached the room, I was already up on the table.

Everything was a blur after that. I do remember that the cleaning lady out in the hall came in and held my hand. It didn't take long for the baby to come, and soon I was back in my bed with my precious new daughter in a little bassinet beside me. She was rosy and plump with shiny black hair. I guess I was about the happiest person to be found. It was cold and rainy outside the window, but so warm and cozy inside. We both slept. When I woke up again, the nurse was checking the baby, and she asked if I was ready to eat. I was more than ready, and she brought in a nice tray of fried chicken, garden peas, rice and gravy, a pear and cottage cheese salad, rolls, and iced tea. I ate, played with my baby, and slept again. By now it was getting dark again, and Dr. Hawes only kept a patient for one night. James was to have already picked me up. It was about eight when he and my sister Eunice walked in. James had worked all day and couldn't leave until he finished his job. The nurse dressed my baby, and Eunice helped me get ready. This made the second time she'd come to take me home from Dr. Hawes. The first time was when I was ten years old and my tonsils had been removed. This time I was a mother with a newborn baby. They had brought a quilt, which they wrapped me and my newborn up in for our trip home. Before leaving the clinic, while the nurse was filling out the baby's forms, Eunice asked me if I had named her yet.

I said, "Yes, I named her Helena, for Mama." She asked me if she could add Judy to her name. That was fine with both me and James, and that's the name she is known by today. The weather was still cold and wet so when we got home, they hustled me and the baby inside and to bed. There was a bright fire in the fireplace, and Edna had scrubbed every floor and really cleaned house for my homecoming. My other three girls crowded around to see their new sister. Red was happy, Mary was curious, and Carolyn was scared of her. She'd never been close to a baby that small before and started to cry. My brother Sam was at his store nearby and also came in to meet the new addition, bringing me the largest ice cream cone I'd ever seen. It looked as though there was every flavor to be had piled on it.

His greeting was, "Hey, remember I told you a long time ago that when I grew up, I was going to have a store and give you an ice cream cone if you behaved yourself. Well, here it is. I guess you behaved." Everybody laughed while I licked away at my reward beside my infant. It was wonderful to be back home and have everything over with. I was happy and content. Lillie Mae, the other cousin who told me fairy tales as a child, had come in and cooked dinner for my family. She worked at the store for Sam. Louis, the boy who lived with us, was trying to quiet Carolyn while Eunice got me and baby settled for the night, but when Jimmy came to take Eunice home, Carolyn went with her. She was getting away from the strange little creature I'd brought home.

The days passed. I was soon up and about, doing my usual tasks. I thought of Mama and smiled when I thought of how horrified she'd be if she could know I was up before the baby was at least two weeks old. I also thought, "Well, Mama I finally got one of my babies named for you."

I had a small squirrel dog named Pee Wee. He made himself Judy's guardian. He'd lie on the floor beside her crib and snarl at anyone who came near except one of the family. Then Papa came home from the hospital. He'd been in for one month. The first mild sunny day, I dressed the baby in some of her prettiest clothes and walked down to my old home for him to see his newest granddaughter. I'll always remember that day. He looked great. His skin was smooth and healthy-looking. His hair was cut short and neat. Sitting in a comfortable chair by the fire, he beamed and held out his arms for Judy. After I'd kissed him and put her in his lap, he asked me what was her name?

"Judy," I said.

"No, no, not that one, what's her other name?"

"Helena," I told him.

He laughed and acted very pleased that I'd named her for Mama. Carolyn had eventually decided to return home but kept her distance from her new sister. Mary, on the other hand, kept a close watch on her, especially when I changed her diaper. She'd stand there watching intently while sucking on her thumb. Finally one day her curiosity got the best of her. Removing her thumb from her mouth, she asked, "Mommy, why her hinny blue?"

"That's her diaper print," I told her. Red was learning to hold her for a few minutes, and so time passed.

Summer came, the days were longer, and Edna and I could get our bunch of children dressed and walk out to the church again. One Sunday morning after breakfast I started getting the girls ready. Red could dress herself and help Mary, so I only had Carolyn and Judy to do for. While combing Carolyn's hair, she fell asleep, so I laid her on the bed to finish with my own dressing and Judy's. All was ready and Carolyn was still sleeping soundly, with her clothes laid out beside her. I hated to wake her up, so James told me to go ahead. He said he'd be home and would watch her. Upon returning from church I found out he'd also fallen asleep. My brother Frank came in holding Carolyn by the hand. He'd been on his way down home and met Carolyn on the road headed toward church in panties, black patent leather shoes and socks, and the rest of her clothes tucked under her arms. He'd asked her where she was going. "Church," she'd told him. That was the last time James babysat for me. Where I went my babies went too. If they couldn't go, we stayed home. I felt that God had put these children in my care and I'd take the best care of them as I could; they were the most precious things in my life.

There've been times when I've met people to discuss my writing, and they've asked me how did I raise my children to adulthood and have them turn out as well as they did. Somehow I never thought of them as something I was raising. To me, they were dear little babies I loved to hold and care for, then little girls I could play games with, tell stories to, dress up pretty, and cook for. They were the center of my life, and I was always thanking God for letting me have them. When they were old enough, they became my friends as well as my children, sharing news of school and their young friends. They would call me Mommie and help with the chores. I tried to teach them ASL, but they preferred fingerspelling and Cued Speech. Communication was never a problem, yet there were some who felt I wouldn't be able to raise children properly and that they would be too much for me. I was urged to let different members of my family have my children and have a tubal ligation done. James asked me where was he supposed to be. Would I give him away too? We laughed over it and went on with our lives.

One by one I watched my little girls go off for their first day of school. James took Mary and Lorey, Edna's oldest child, for their school shots and to register for school. Mary entered Teachey Elementary School, where Red was a fourth-grader. Lorey went to C. W. Dobbins Elementary School. Mary, too, loved school and learned quickly. In third grade she recited "The Night Before Christmas" all the way through without making any mistakes.

Soon it was time for Carolyn to start school. Back then children took lots of pride in how they looked when going to school, especially the first day. For Carolyn's first day I wanted her to look especially nice. I chose a rose-colored dress with ruffles and lace, with matching bows and socks. She looked like a doll. Watching them get on the bus, I noticed the two older girls were very careful and protective of their younger sister. I was so proud of all of them. I smiled and cried at the same time. Judy, my baby, was the only one left with me. I couldn't wait for the bus to come in that evening to ask Carolyn how she'd fared and whether she liked school. She came in very quietly and answered my questions as to who her teacher was. It was the same one Red and Mary had had in first grade, Thelma Thompson, my cousin's wife.

All the children from first through twelfth grade rode the same bus, and a high school student was the bus driver. They'd drop the younger kids off at the elementary school then drive to their high school (Charity High School) with the rest. Since my house was closest to the road, the other kids nearby gathered there to meet the bus. Judy would watch them get on the bus and watch as the bus pulled off. As soon as it was out of sight, she'd race to my coffee table, clear everything off, and set it with her tea set, then place all of her dolls and stuffed animals around it, and say they were having a tea party. So I had to carry them cookies and milk or cocoa. She'd already eaten her breakfast with her sisters before they left for school. She was a happy child and played peacefully while I did my morning chores, cleaning the kitchen, making beds, and sweeping. Sometimes when I'd finish my chores, we'd walk someplace, maybe to Edna's if she was home. She would sometimes stay in town at her mother Janie's house, because her children attended C. W. Dobbins Elementary School. I missed her greatly when she was away. At other times we went across the field to see Lattice or down home to see Papa when we knew he was there. He'd recovered from his heart attack and was on the go as much as ever. I also enjoyed visiting Mrs. Lizzie Bland and her sister Artelia, who lived right down the road a little ways.

We still went to church when the weather was pleasant enough for us to walk. We had a little black and white dog name Pete, who felt he was as much family as anyone else. Pee Wee had gotten killed. Pete followed us everywhere. If we left him in the house, he'd break a windowpane and get out to wait beside the road for us to return. If we left him tied outside, he'd get loose somehow, break a windowpane, and go back in the house. When we would get back, the first thing we would see was his head sticking out the window where the pane had been, waiting for us with his tongue hanging out like he was laughing at us. One Sunday we tied him with what I thought was really strong rope, and went to church. It was a warm summer day, so the church doors were open. We had no air conditioning then. Reverend Wright was just getting into his sermon when I saw people's heads turning or looking at their feet and lifting their feet. I wondered what was happening but didn't have long to wonder. Something pressed against my leg. It was Pete! He'd gnawed the rope and freed himself then tracked us to the church, where he came in and went through all those feet until he found mine. One of our deacons, James Arthur, shooed him out, but back he came, and this time took up his post on the floor right in front of the pulpit, in sight of everyone, and proceeded to scratch his fleas. He then went to sleep. Reverend Wright had seen him often enough to know who he belonged to and said to leave him alone. He stayed for the whole service. Every afternoon at the exact time the school bus was due, he'd get up and go to the door so he could be let outside to wait for the bus, looking down the road anxiously until he saw it coming.

Although Papa had recovered from his illness, he still couldn't farm as he'd once done, so he'd sold most of the land and built another little house over in Pender County, not far from Eunice and Jimmy's home. It was so sad seeing the last person leaving the old homeplace, but he came over often and still went down there, but it just wasn't the same. As long as he lived and was able, he'd still come by with hoes and rakes for me to go with him to clean and work around Mama's grave and their little boy's.

Lots of things changed, as they always do, but Cousin Bert was still a regular overnight visitor. I'd put a let-out couch in my living room so she'd have a comfortable place to sleep. One cold day in January she'd gotten some turnip greens from somewhere and asked if she could cook them at my house. I said, "Sure," so, she set about happily cooking her dinner, a full course meal with meat and bread as well. She ate a big supper and seemed to enjoy it so much. Afterward she took her shoes off and settled in a comfortable chair near the wood heater and listened while I read and discussed the Bible stories with my children. Then I started to get them ready for bed.

Mary had taken off her shoes, and I had Judy on my lap to get her ready for bed when Red noticed something about Cousin Bert and told me to look at her. I looked and saw that both legs were stretched straight out in front of her, with her head resting on the back of the chair and hands across her stomach. Alarmed, I sat Judy on the floor and ran to her, calling, "Cousin Bert, Cousin Bert!" No response. I took her shoulders and tried to pull her to a sitting position, but she seemed to be too stiff. My children had all run into their bedroom and slammed the door. I ran out in the front yard and lifted my voice to high heaven screaming for help, hoping nearby neighbors would hear me and come. No one did. I started back into the house and met my children coming out at full speed. They passed me heading for I don't know where. Looking down, I saw my baby girl trotting along beside me. Picking her up and putting her on my hip, I tried to catch up with the other three. I could see they had turned the corner and gone down the road heading to William Boney's house. I followed, but when I reached the corner, I was just in time to see light coming from William's front door and my girls disappearing inside. I broke into a trot rounding the curve and fell right into the ditch. Judy had both arms locked around my neck and both legs around my waist. She didn't even come loose when I fell, except to use one hand to pound my back and say, "Get up, Mommy, get up."

"How am I going to get up with you strangling me?" I asked her. I finally managed to crawl back out with her intact on my back. By the time we reached William's house, he'd called his brother, Albert Henry, next door. His wife, Melissa, was with him. They put me and my children in their cars and drove back to my house. Cousin Bert had come around, but she was sick to her stomach. She didn't even know what had happened to her. Mrs. Lizzie, Artelia, and Sadie had also come over. They cleaned Cousin Bert and everything up and told her they'd take her to her daughter's house out on the highway where she could get to a doctor if need be. It took me and the girls a long time to feel settled enough to go to bed. We waited up for James and Louis to come home. I was horrified to find that Mary and Carolyn didn't have on shoes when they had run down to William Boney's house. Mary did have on socks, but Carolyn didn't have on socks or shoes. Red assured me that Carolyn would be all right because she and Mary each had her hands and had run so fast they kept her feet lifted off the ground. After that Cousin Bert spent only one night with me. The children were uneasy even then and kept looking and listening to see if she was still breathing. Mrs. Mary Hayes, her daughter, kept her at her house from then on. Her health declined, and she was never able to walk the road and enjoy being out as she had once done. Poor Cousin Bert, we had come to love her, and the children said she was the closest they had to a grandmother. The last time I visited her before she died, she asked about Judy. I will always remember Cousin Bert. She lost her sight a year or so before she died.

It seemed no time before my baby girl was trudging out to get on the bus with her sisters. By now Red was graduating from Teachey Elementary and entering Charity High School. She promptly signed up to be a cheerleader. The year Carolyn was in first grade, her teacher announced that Christmas that she wouldn't be coming back after the holidays because she was being transferred to another school near Greensboro, which was a good distance away. Carolyn didn't think her teacher could be replaced, so she announced she would be graduating from Teachey School and wouldn't be coming back either. Of course she did go back and loved her new teacher, Mrs. Darden, just as much as her other teacher if not more. I liked her too. She seemed to be a very nice person. She would ask me if she could take Carolyn home with her for the weekend. They went to a church where some of the people got happy and were shouting. Carolyn shouted too, but her shouts were from fright, and she didn't go back again. She continued to love Mrs. Darden. She brought her pet rabbits to school and made learning fun, but she was only there for one year.

Red made lots of friends in school, both boys and girls, and so did Mary. Carolyn was a different story. She made friends with little girls—among them were Patricia Flowers and Geraldine Sloan—but she didn't seem to like the boys. They'd tease her and she'd fight back. A few years later, when Red was driving the bus, she said when she pulled into Teachey Elementary to pick up the children, the first thing she saw was her sister Carolyn having a fight with a little boy. Red jumped off the bus to go see about her, but she needn't have worried. Carolyn had torn all the buttons off his shirt, and he was getting the worst of the deal; also, Mr. Larkin, the principal, ran where they were and got ahold of the boy. The boy was larger than Carolyn and had been picking on her.

Through the years all of the school personnel had gotten to know me. They also knew I was a seamstress and asked me to come to school with my girls and make costumes for school plays. I was asked to teach a fourth-grade class to knit, crochet, and sew simple things. I baked cakes for class parties and made white graduation dresses for the eighth-grade girls.

It felt good to be part of my children's schooldays. It was fun, too. Mrs. Larkin, the principal's wife, taught the eighth-grade class. She worked so hard to upgrade the school. It was a very old school. Each year the eighth-grade class raised money to leave a gift for the school. They furnished bricks and had a walk built from the front steps to the driveway where the bus stopped. Another class paid for a water fountain that was placed in the front hall, and another class bought a flagpole and flag. They only had outhouses at the school, so Mrs. Larkin had a new addition built onto the school. Now they had a lunchroom and restrooms. They'd been eating lunch in a classroom.

All the work and planning for the school made it seem as if we were all one big family. Everybody knew each other. When I'd be at the school sewing, I used the auditorium to sew in, and every child or teacher passing through always had a smile and would say, "Hey, Mrs. Wright." Some of them would stop to see if I wanted a glass of water or a snack. I also ate lunch with them.

Once they started integrating the schools, Teachey Elementary was closed, and the children were bused to other schools. I was never a part of any of the other schools. I just knew the teachers who taught my children. I did get to see Red graduate from Charity High School and Mary from Teachey Elementary. The ceremonies were held on the same Sunday. Mary's was first, and then we rushed to Charity to see Red's. No one will ever know just how I felt the sunny Sunday afternoon in May, seeing Mary in her white dress and all the kids gathered around the old piano while Mrs. Wallace played. Mr. Larkin and all the visiting dignitaries sat in a row on the stage. It was beautiful. Through Mrs. Larkin's efforts they had finally gotten red velvet stage curtains, and pots of flowers dressed everything up. My eyes were full. I had been coming to this school for over eight years, and I knew it would never be the same. Some of us had already received letters about changing schools. At least Mary would be at Charity for a while, but my two little ones would be going to Wallace Elementary school when school opened again. I am so glad my sister got to see my girls graduate that Sunday. I was so proud and wanted to share them with her.

When we got to Charity, Eunice couldn't sit with me because they had reserved seats for parents only. I sat alone (James had to go to work). Then I heard, or felt, the vibrations from the drums start up. There was one in the hall right by the entrance. They were playing the drums as the kids marched in, one at a time. It was a steady beat. Red was the third one. I turned my head to watch her marching in, her cap jaunty. She gave me a quick look and a smile when she passed. The class had composed their own song. It was "Oh Charity High, We Love You So," sung to the tune of "Danny Boy." Their colors were maroon and gold. I'd made her a simple pink silk dress with rows of lace down the front to wear under her robe. Her robe was white. I thought of Mama and my own graduation, and I knew she would have been just as proud of my two girls on that Sunday evening. I hoped that somehow or other she saw them.

The last photograph taken of the six Herring children. Background, left to right, Sam, Bennie, Frank and Willie; foreground, Eunice and me.

# 22

# A New Time

*If you can dream—and not make dreams your master,*
*If you can think—and not make thoughts your aim;*
*If you can meet with Triumph and Disaster*
*And treat those two impostors just the same.*

Rudyard Kipling,
"If"

THERE'S not much to tell about the girls' school days after they changed schools. Mary was at Charity for three years, then it was changed to a middle school for seventh- and eighth-graders. After that they had to go to Wallace–Rose Hill High School, the formerly all-white school. It seemed no one was happy with the new system. There were bomb scares and other incidents. Even so, Mary went to the new school and graduated at the top of her class. She won some scholarships, and entered UNC-Greensboro, where she did four years' work in three years. Then it was Carolyn's year to march. After she graduated, she went to Washington, D.C., to live with Red, who had married two months after her graduation, gone to business school, then worked while her husband fought in the Vietnam war. He was wounded, and I thought he was dead the way Red had fits. When he was able, she met him in Hawaii, so that boosted her spirits. Upon his return they moved to Kentucky to finish out his time in service and then moved to South Carolina for a year or so, where they became parents of a baby girl, Tracy Lynette, my first grandbaby.

Papa got to see at least one of my grandchildren, then he too passed on. Red had just been home for a visit and taken the baby to see him. She and Carolyn had just gone back to D.C. when they had to come back home that same week for Papa's funeral. He had an appointment to go into town to get his new eyeglasses and was sitting by the TV waiting for one of Bennie's girls to come pick him up, when he just leaned back in his chair and died just that quick. I'm thankful he didn't have to suffer a long time. Although he lived in Pender County and I didn't get to see him as often as before, I felt lost with him and Mama both gone. Eunice and I sat on her bed and cried together. She'd been closer to Papa, and I knew she hurt badly. The morning after his funeral I woke up and just lay there thinking about Papa and how he used to tickle my feet to wake me up. It seemed like I could feel his presence and his telling me to get up and do something and to stop grieving. Without telling anyone else, I dressed, went outside, got my hoe and some yard flowers and went to Mama's grave, worked around it, threw the old flowers away and put fresh ones on it, then I felt better.

It seemed like the years were flying by now. All of the little kids I've been writing about are either grown-up or teenagers. Some are in college, and some married with babies of their own. Bennie had six daughters—Shirley, Della, Dorothy, Mary Alice, Mable Lee (Pig), and Sandy the baby girl. She and Judy were about the same age. Frank also had six children—Marion (Nod), Maxine, Bennie Louise (Cootie), Lillie Carol, and two boys Lloyd (Jimrod), and James Edward (Duke). Willie had two, Billy and Diana, and Sam had two, Bonita and Mike. Eunice was the only one without children, but she mothered her nieces and nephews.

Her house was always full of young people. And although the kids who'd hung out at my house were also grown-up, they still came by often. They enjoyed talking with James. June Boney and his sister Rachel were married and each had two children. June had a little girl, Yvette, and a son, Marcellus, and Rachel had two daughters, Pam and Nicole. I had the pleasure of babysitting their children as well as Lillie Carol's children, Mickey, Daryl, and Rodney. I was proud that they trusted me with the most precious things they had. My children were still young enough to get a kick out of playing with them.

Iron Mine, too, was changing along with its people. Our little two-room schoolhouse, where I'd first made acquaintance with "education" and spent so many happy hours, had been torn down, and a neat white house replaced it. This was now the home of Mary Frances and Sam Pratt. She'd been one of the big girls when I was a beginner. The little white wood church had been enlarged and bricked in. The woods beside it that had run all the way down to Cousin Mamie's house had been cut up into lots and sold to whoever wanted to buy them. The old homeplace wasn't the same. I loved it still, but looking at all the familiar fields and woods every day brought back too many memories of those who'd been dear to me and were no longer there. Also, the roads were all dirt, and during bad weather the roads turned to mud, making it hard for the school buses and other cars to travel on. A lot of neighbors were buying up those lots like hotcakes. Frank had bought one as soon as they went up for sale. These were choice homesites that a lot of people had wanted to buy a piece of for years, but the owner refused to sell. Then she sold the land to a well-to-do man, and he divided it into 150-by-300-foot lots and sold them to anybody who wanted to buy one and was able to pay.

I already had the old homeplace, but it was isolated, and I wanted the children to live on a better road. So being me, with not much money but a whole lot of faith, I used what I did have for a down payment. I trusted God and my ability to work to be able to pay the rest. James didn't want to move away from where we lived. He loved the old place and wanted to rebuild there. Mr. Price, the man selling the lots, gave me the time I needed to pay for the land. With the good Lord behind me, I sewed, fixed tax papers, tied and graded tobacco, and had the place paid for in a few months. When James saw I was determined to get a house on it, he came in with me on a loan, so it wasn't long before we had a nice little three-bedroom house with bath and everything. Those things had just come to the rural areas. You can imagine how excited and happy we were to move in. Eunice came over to help me get settled in and put up curtains, and so on. She was almost as excited as the rest of us.

The next evening Carolyn and I walked back out to the old place to get a few more things we'd left, including our cat. As we were leaving and got a little ways down the road, we looked back. It was a cold January evening, and the sun was setting so clear and beautiful. The house looked deserted and lonely, outlined against the evening sky. We stopped, and I told her it seemed as if I should be in the kitchen getting ready to call them to supper. She said yes, and that smoke should be coming from the chimney and she and Judy playing in their favorite spot on the ditch bank. All at once I felt as if I was leaving my babies behind and a part of us all. We stood there and cried in the cold winter air. However, once back in our bright warm new home, we were soon happy again. Our dog Pete refused to sleep in the new house, so I built him a little house near the kitchen door. He'd go back to his old haunts when he felt like it. One day I was digging in the yard, setting out some plants, when Pete came up dragging a long piece of vine in his mouth and set it down at my feet.

"Well, Pete, did you bring me something to set out?" I asked him.

He wagged his tail, so I took it, thinking it was just something he'd found, and stuck it in a hole anyway. When spring came and things started budding, his vine did too, to my surprise. It not only budded it bloomed and turned out to be a piece of wisteria vine that had grown over the end of the porch at the old place. It's been years, and Pete's gone, but the vine is still growing and blooming and I think of Pete. He was the third dog I had owned since Queen who seemed like a part of the family.

It was much easier on the girls to be living near the highway. They could stay inside on cold mornings waiting for the bus. They could take part in Sunday school and church work. Mary and Carolyn sang in the junior choir, and Judy sang with the children. It was something she was proud of and marched in with her head held high, and singing with gusto. Mrs. Annie Hayes was her Sunday school teacher. We also went to prayer meeting on Wednesday night and Baptist Training Union on Sunday evenings. Usually the only adults were Harding Thompson and James Arthur Hayes, both deacons. Another of the girls who grew up playing with my girls, Gwen Murphy, started teaching the juniors. She was a good teacher and they loved her. Angelene Bennett was our secretary, and Mary started putting programs and plays together. Every year near Christmas, I can once again see us headed for the church on a cold December night walking close, with arms linked for warmth. Against the cold, clear sky and bright stars, it seemed like I could hear the song "O Holy Night." Those are beautiful memories.

Sometimes at book signings someone will ask me what I miss hearing the most. It's always music and birds singing in the woods on a clear morning. At times, I still hear it with my heart and in memory. There are some things we don't ever lose.

Things do change, and the years seem to fly by. It seemed when the children entered high school, they just marched through and were out in no time, either going to college or working. Mary entered UNC–Greensboro, and Angelene and Gwen went to Winston-Salem State University. Carolyn and Priscilla, Gwen's sister, had a little more high school to deal with.

I was so proud of our young people. It wasn't many years ago that it was an impossibility, or at best a very hard struggle, for Black children to go to college. Now, where there was a will to go, there was also a way. Bonita was enrolled at UNC–Chapel Hill. Bonnie Thompson, Harding's daughter, went to Winston-Salem, and Edna's daughter Lorey went to A&T in Greensboro. Sheila went to a school in Florida and Nick to North Carolina State in Raleigh.

I wish I could say I've seen some of my old schoolmates and that I know how they're doing. But being that I'm the only deaf person in this area, the only ones I've seen since school days are my old friends and play sisters, Flossie Johnson and Nell Kerr. They're both married, and it's Flossie Everette and Nell McCauley now. They both moved away but have relatives here. I don't know Flossie's husband, but Nell's husband went to school in Raleigh. Flossie has four children, including one girl, whom she named Mary, and three boys. The oldest boy became the first Black police officer in Wallace. They live in Fayetteville, North Carolina.

After finishing business school and moving to D.C. with her husband and baby, Red started working at Gallaudet University. When I visited her there, I met lots of deaf people. It was amazing. It's a big beautiful campus, and everyone signs, so you don't know who is hearing and who isn't. There are plenty of Black students, and they can take courses in anything offered at colleges for hearing people. There I met and made friends with Marie Boland, who is deaf, from upstate New York. She worked there as manager of the main lunchroom. Red's boss was also deaf and worked as manager of the bookstore. This was Ronald Suttcliff. There were so many distinguished-looking people with nice homes and families, driving their own cars on Washington's busy streets I was awestruck. It made me wonder what my life would have been like if I had been able to go to school here.

And at last I was accepted at Gallaudet. I was awarded an honorary degree in the spring of 2004. I've also taken part in conferences there and have met many people who have been wonderful—from President I. King Jordan on. It's a beautiful place with beautiful people and I feel a part of it now. I've truly been blessed.

I've always believed there's a higher one who lays out the course we are to follow, and I guess I'm following the course he laid for me. I am not displeased with my life, and I feel thankful it turned out as well as it did. I'm satisfied with it and proud of my children and grandchildren. Who knows what else is in store for me?

Linda, me, and Mary on my day of joy and pride, May 14, 2004, when I was awarded an honorary bachelor of arts degree from Gallaudet University.